Rose PARADISE
Essays of Fathoming

Gurdjieff, The Mahatmas, Andreev,
The Emerald Tablets, OASPHE, and More

Frankie Pauling Hutton

ISBN 978-1-64468-847-2 (Paperback)
ISBN 978-1-64468-848-9 (Digital)

Covenant Books, Inc.
11661 Hwy 707
Murrells Inlet, SC 29576
www.covenantbooks.com

..."That island on which Mister God Himself
and the deserving souls exist is called "paradise,"
and existence there is just "Roses, Roses."

Gurdjieff's Beelzebub's Tales to His Grandson
Ch. 20, p. 217, First Series

Frontis

CONTENTS

INTRODUCTION TO
ROSE PARADISE

The red rose is the lodestar flower on Earth planet and the essays in this collection reveal why. These essays represent the portfolio of mostly non-botanical aspects of unarguably the world's most revered, hyped and diversely used flower, a gift to the human species. Very likely a global first, this synthesis-collection delves exclusively into the mystical, literary, semiotic and some medicinal qualities of the indomitable rose. This is no small feat. Research and writing of the essays span geographic time lines, cultures and epochs to tell the arcane story of what I've come to believe is the most important flower of human existence. There are many prisms from which to view the rose and the five essays contained here provide essential insight, with validation over vast time lines, to answer lingering questions about why this lovely exotic flower was put in our midst. For me, the real messages of the red rose have become clearer and clearer. Now it has become possible to provide strident reasoning and substantiation about the urgency of the rose's presence on earth for contemporary humans. I have always recognized the rose as lovely and unusual, but wondered about its presence in our midst as perhaps the most profound flower rendering on earth.

These essays reveal potentially life enhancing messages: first, the rose has an undeniable connection to mysticism, to the ineffable. And, what's more, there is no flower on earth like the rose as it has been embraced—that is to say co-opted in diverse ways globally by remarkably talented, well educated, intuitive humans. People, places, things and groups are named after this perfect flower.

Brilliant individuals surveyed here have unique connections to the rose. In a distinct, singular class, they have all managed to leave behind work and genius connected to the flower that spans decades and is indeed a feast for the mind. The fact that the rose has been used by a bevy of bright people in extraordinary ways underscores its uniqueness as a treasured gift from the Divine. Each of the people fortunate enough to have encountered the mystical rose has been propelled to wide, lasting acclaim in some measure and yet their stories have never been told in a continuum or connected way. The purpose of this book is to accomplish this synthetic feat and more.

Those special humans who have known ultra qualities of the rose left behind a trail of evidence for us as to its importance. For instance, writing the **Divine Comedy** in the late Middle Ages Dante embraced the rose as an urgent mystical symbol in his timeless epic poem. Nostradamus' discovery of the medicinal qualities of the rose during 16th century France's bout with the black plague rings out as one of the most remarkable medical feats known to humans up to that time. More recently, the rose has been embraced by Daniel Andreev's secret writing of his masterpiece **Rose of the World** from inside a gulag in early 20th century Russia. The saga of Dr. Harada, a medical physician and world-class surgeon, who began the rose garden movement in Japan after the World War II is a touching, treasured story introduced here. The flower's use in the writings of G. I. Gurdjieff is strategically well planted for those who follow or have been curious about the remarkably superior higher consciousness tradition he left behind. Although mentioned only briefly in Gurdjieff's **Beelzebub's Tales to His Grandson**, the true meaning of the rose in connection to Paradise or the quest for eternal life is amplified in his last uncompleted chapter in *Life is Real Only Then, When 'I Am.'* Likewise, the flower is planted in an extraordinary lyric composition of C.A. Miles and has been used or embraced by others such as Helena P. Blavatsky—all bespeaking mystical, otherworldly qualities of the flower. In these thought-provoking essays, we meet all of these extraordinary individuals and more. Herewith are reflections on practical, intuitive and symbiotic work of well-known humans and of others, not so well known but still important to a new discipline that I will graciously anoint: "rose studies." There are deep reasons for the rose's presence on earth but most people will never fathom the gist or truly understand these reasons. The revelations put forth here become clearer and clearer when one is ready to "hear" the messages. In this regard, the introduction to *Rose Lore*, the forerunner and companion to these essays, reminds readers "above us, nearly out of sight, is the most provocative evidence of the rose's importance: the rose nebula known by NASA (the United States' National Aeronautical and Space Administration) as NGC 2244. Four thousand five hundred light years away in the cosmos, this vibrant nebula hovers over the earth in the shape of a red rose as if underscoring messages of the flower from above. Why is it there? After all, this incredible nebula might have taken on many other shapes or forms too numerous to mention. Provocatively, for some of us to see and be aware, the shape is a red rose!

The first three essays contained here were published originally by Rowman-Littlefield in my first rose-related brainchild, an edited book-anthology titled *Rose Lore: Essays in Cultural History and Semiotics.* Those diverse-authored essays were also subsequently published under the same title in an abridged version as an audio book CD, in paper cover second and third editions by UNCUT Voices Press, Frankfurt, Germany and finally translated by an exceptional team of scholars at China Women's University and published in the mandarin language by Peking University Press. The last two essays were researched and written in a later time frame, between 2016–2020, and are just now made available.

Appreciation goes to a few colleagues and supporters who have facilitated research and writing of all of these essays. It was Leonard Jackson in Baltimore, Maryland, for instance, who first introduced me to the rose nebula and

Michael Maciopa in New Jersey who pressed me many years ago to devote time to study *The Emerald Tablets*. Others, no less important in the quest to learn the way of the rose, have been named in three editions of *Rose Lore.* The original contributors to that anthology did their rosy best at research to help me educate readers about various cultural and geographically diverse aspects of the flower. Especially, Tobe Levin and Alexander Prodovikov felt the project of general public education about the multi-faceted rose from the beginning, over a decade ago, and have both offered valuable, continued assistance. Dr. Levin often thanks me for introducing her to ultra aspects of the rose and sends me rose inspired post cards from around the world of her travels. I thank her for the myriad ways she has facilitated the project. More recently, Stephen Popiotek, Tatyana Koponova, Joel Sunbear, John Grebe and Evan Hutton have offered assistance and feedback as first "public readers" of the last two essays for which I am honored and grateful. The encouragement and support of my late husband, Vernon O'Meally was steadfast and unflinching during years of research.

Continued rosy thanks to members of the Maryland, Deerfield Beach, Florida and Surya Study Group, New Jersey of the Theosophical Society of America is appropriate. Likewise, members of the Abraxis Theosophical Lodge in Pennsylvania asked the right questions to keep me focused on the trail of metaphysical rose research. Those groups together have provided a magnificent training ground and shown genuine interest in my rose lectures and workshops that has propelled me to continue research, learn more and grow up fully in my understanding of this quintessential flower. In particular, executive board members of The Maryland Theosophical Lodge, Baltimore, have been stalwart in offering a continued haven of support to the *Rose Project*, my extraordinary brainchild and an outgrowth of the original rose book, a collection, now in print for more than a decade on three continents. I dedicate this book to all of them, to the memory of my parents Frank and Georgia Pauling and also to the contributors of various editions of *Rose Lore*, the precursor to this book.

Frankie Pauling Hutton, Ph. D.

www.roseproject.com

Chapter One

"Dying Laughing"
The Rose From Yeats to Rumi

We lovers laugh to hear "This should be
more that and that should be more this"
coming from people sitting in a wagon
tilted in a ditch. Going in search of the
heart, I found a huge rose under my feet,
and roses under all our feet...

Rumi

(Translation by Coleman Barks)

This essay surveys timeless, metaspiritual qualities of the
rose as reflected in classical poetry and literature. Serving as
didactic guideposts for human beings, the renderings considered here should be no stranger to sophisticated academic

communities. Yet and still the higher underlying messages are not so obvious. The passages to be considered in this essay transcend vast time periods and places to teach esoteric knowledge to those seekers who are awake and aware. Thus, from important distinctly singular writers of diverse cultures and epochs, we are presented with the same messages in different format and creative style. A bevy of metaphysically astute writers have used the rose as a potent symbol to fashion poems and short stories that provide insight to higher consciousness. The writers whose work is surveyed here apparently knew full well that the rose is an exceptional symbol "planted" on earth to teach all who are ready to fathom the gist about real life, death, and higher spiritual realms. The rose is unlike human guides who appear at strategic times when one is on the path; it is ever present, ever ready, ever useful and ever beautiful for those who are wise enough to pay attention to it.

Intriguingly, because no one knows for sure exactly when the rose first appeared on earth, the lovely flower has come to have the staying power and clout of such enduring symbols as the cross, the oceans, the sun, mountains and so on. Eons ago, although we cannot be sure precisely when, the quintessential rose took its place beside entities that far overstep the material mind toward the ineffable and everlasting. Explored in this essay as a profound metaphor in timeless literature and poetry, the rose easily, pervasively transcends what is known of its potent botanical qualities. For it is in treading timeless literature connected with this magnificent flower that it can be revealed in full splendor. Careful review and reflection of rose-embracing literature and poetry reveals that the flower in all its perfection is a direct link to the Source of all and everything. For those who have eyes to see, it comes into focus as one of the most long lasting, widely used and beautifully powerful symbols of all time.

Known for its beauty, medicinal qualities and as a provocative organization, club,[1] and municipal[2] symbol for eons, the rose has also been a powerful metaphor in movies[3], in dance[4] and in works of fiction and nonfiction.[5] Barbara Seward's study of the rose in British literature is used pivotally here to reinforce the notion of the flower's wide use in popular literature. Allegorically and metaphysically, some of the works used in Seward's literary analysis are selections that transcend the material world. Surely she was aware of this. In *The Symbolic Rose* Seward uses Dante Alighiere's *Divine Comedy* as the primal literary antecedent to engineer a skillful analysis of the rose in selected works of British authors William Butler Yeats (1865–1939), T. S. Eliot (1888–1965) and James Joyce (1882–1941), all masters of prose and poetry. Seward goes further to make the point that before Dante's *Divine Comedy* "no earlier writer had attempted to express through a single rose the diversity of meanings associated with" the flower.[6] Likewise, Seward proffers that no one "had demonstrated the poetic genius" or fully reconciled "such seemingly disparate qualities as carnal and spiritual love." Clearly, Seward did not reach back far enough into the vast history and cultures of the globe to take note that the rose has been used in mystically fired literature long before William Butler Yeats and even long before Dante's *Divine Comedy*. What's more, it is apparent that Yeats was aware of the rose's connection to the Divine for he often wrote about both as corollaries.

In the *Symbolic Rose*, Seward, herself a British author, introduces Yeats's work from a nineteenth century foundation of theosophy and secret societies while Eliot and Joyce "acquire a good part of their meaning from associations with the rose of Dante…"—that is to say from Italy of the 14th century. Apparently all three author's works were influenced by

Dante Alighieri's *Divine Comedy* simply because it is a masterpiece. The story is a classic in world literature and has been used as a teaching tool in the academy for hundreds of years, but mastering *The Divine Comedy* is no easy feat and there is no attempt to accomplish its complete analysis here except to make clear that Dante's journey points to what Helen Luke has described as toward the "vision of God" and the single truth that "without divinity there can be no conscious humanity and without humanity the divine remains an abstraction."[7] This point will be underscored in various ways in this and in the essays following. A short recap of Alighieri and his *Divine Comedy* is useful here to show the epic poem's connection to the symbol of the rose. Under the influence of the Roman Church, Dante Alighieri's inner struggle was profound as was his exile from Florence between 1307 and 1321, the time during which the epic poem known as *Divine Comedy* was written. The exile, simply put, was the result of bad political and church politics of the time. The ruling political party, Guelphs, were supported by Dante's family, but split over the nature and power of the papacy. This divide resulted in a lasting feud in which Dante who is said to be one of the world's oldest poets, protested papal policies. Battles between the two groups went on for years and Alighieri went into extended exile.

Dante Alighieri's sets his saga to begin during the Easter Season on Good Friday in the year 1300 and tells of a man on a journey in which he encounters characters and symbols related to salvation and damnation. Significantly, the entire work is based on the number three, an important number in metaphysics that suggests human beings must rise above the dualities confronting them in this world to a higher place that is sans tension, fighting and foolishness. Thus, in sacred geometry when a third force is introduced, two initial forces are neutralized. On his journey Dante is "turned back by three beasts—the leopard, the lion and the wolf—by his love of pleasure, by his fierce pride, and by the terrifying latent greed and avarice of the ego."[8] These are "beasts" that most of us have to conquer on the material realm, in what we refer to as "life," in order to move up and on to the Divine. Verses in *Divine Comedy* are arranged in units of three lines and the epic is composed of three books, *Inferno, Purgatory* and *Paradise,* all phases Dante encounters on his spiritual journey.[9] Stiff moral judgments are forced on Dante as he reaches Earthly Paradise. In paradise, Dante encounters Beatrice, the sacred feminine, his guide and inspiration. It is she who guides him toward God, revealed in "an ineffable vision of light."[10] Of course paradise is a beautiful place where the atmosphere is in "perfect society moving in the harmony of the dance or forming the flawless pattern of the *rose*."[11] It's easy to follow Dante's symbolism here, to imagine the rose as heavenly perfection.

Dante waited until near the end of the epic to introduce the symbolism of the rose probably for that reason, "heaven" does symbolize perfection for which we must strive as we work toward conquering the "beasts" of the material realm. Overcoming the dualities of the earth to the point that a third force is introduced is not work for the weak at heart; it is daily work that must be done in earnest all the time, twenty-four-seven to use contemporary vernacular. And, depending on the progress made this time around, perhaps the striving continues in other incarnations as well. In Canto XXXII, Dante spells out, in seven steps or gradations the struggles one must endure to reach paradise, leaf by leaf as "throned on the rose." In this last Canto, Dante is really on to something profound that has been somewhat veiled from the masses for thousands of years. Actually, it hasn't been hidden too deeply for as we will take note in the next chapter the knowledge is replete in sacred books and works globally, the most prominent of which is the Christian *Holy Bible* and in a variety of literature, including significant works of fiction. To stay on point, the pathway is mapped for those who work to undertake the journey through consistent work that revolves around unconditional love, service and the untiring desire to know themselves and truth.

As a symbol, the rose continues to be a marker on the pathway. The initiated know well as do those with long traditions of meditation and study in metaphysics have some sense that the phrase "leaf by leaf" alludes to the consecrated work that must be done individually, unremittingly to move up the ladder, through the full number of rounds to connect fully and everlastingly with what Christianity has labeled the Holy Spirit. This process has been laid out and even described in sacred literature such as in T*he Christian Holy Bible* to be considered later, but it is also deeply hermetic knowledge that is easy to miss for the spiritually uninspired. Dante was inspired and wanted very much to be illumined. For as both writer and protagonist of *The Divine Comedy*, Dante Alighieri's epic underscores the pain and the beasts of life that we all encounter. His earthly or material body ended in Revenna in

1321 while away from his beloved Florence. If Dante didn't make the full journey to eternal life or endlessness, his poem shows us that he was intimately acquainted with the path and knew of the impediments to reaching the Light. His epic has been and continues to be a staple in world literature[12], religious studies and philosophy. Peter Bondanella's analysis has shown that Dante Alighieri "was under the influence of Saint Jerome's Latin Vulgate version of the Holy Bible from which he draws 600 references to the epic poem. Alighieri, according to Bondanella's view, confronts the seven deadly sins of lust, gluttony, avarice, sloth, wrath, envy and pride in purgatory.[13]

Although the work of the three authors Seward considered in her analysis speaks volumes about love, life, eternity, resolution and ultimately connection to the Source, it is Yeats's metaphysical connections that tip us off that his objective is much higher, to teach us something about full initiation, interestingly in the tradition of the rose as the ultimate metaphor, just as expressed by Dante Alighieri. Relatively, Yeats uses the rose a lot in his poems and short stories; it appears in "To the Rose Upon the Rood of Time," "The Rose of the World," "The Rose of Peace." The urgent rose metaphor is used by Yeats skillfully and quietly in allegory, metaphor and symbol throughout his written work. The question is why? Well, it is apparent from all we know about Yeats at this remove that he grew tremendously in understanding of mysticism. At times he seems to want his readers to know this and just as important, to tip them off that growth is possible for them too.

While Yeats's use of the rose appears to be the most esoteric of the three authors Seward explored, it should be noted tangentially that Seward also does a fine analysis of Eliot and Joyce's use of the flower. Where the work of T. S. Eliot is concerned, she shows that the rose is the "obvious symbol of whole and enduring resolution" even as it combines "the romanticism of a yearning, nostalgic, insatiable age with absolute, authoritarian standards of medieval times..."[14] Known for social criticism in both his essays and poetry, Eliot was born in St. Louis, Missouri (1888) and educated at Harvard University. He moved to England after taking his master's degree in 1910, thus he is sometimes claimed as a favorite son by both the United States and England; obviously Seward includes him in the latter geographic lot. James Joyce was educated at Jesuit schools in Dublin and after 1902 moved to England. He also lived in Zurich during World War I; but the extremes of the two—that is a solid catholic education pitted against the backdrop of the horrors of a world war must have been very difficult for his psyche. Seward notes the conflict in his writing. The whole point is that all three great writers Yeats, Eliot and Joyce made full use of the rose in their prose and verse.

Clearly Yeats' use of the rose in one particular short story is the centerpiece of this essay. His prose treads higher spiritual realms in a timeless but brief story that is easy to recount here and easily instructive. Eruditely reasoned, Seward's analysis says that Yeats's work is a marker in the literary history of the rose. For it is Yeats Seward proffers who makes the first successful attempt since Dante's *Divine Comedy* to express tradition as well as personal meanings in the single symbol of the rose. Seward notes that Yeats used a "medley of artistic and religious concepts."[15] It is apparent that Seward was aware when she wrote *The Symbolic Rose* that Yeats had joined the Dublin Theosophical Society in 1886 and followed this association with the hermetic tradition of the Order of the Golden Dawn in London, then a highly intellectual secret fraternity.[16] The influence of the Theosophical Society on Yeats was probably as profound as this initiation into the Hermetic Order of the Golden Dawn, said to be an offshoot of the Rosicrucians, another secret order established perhaps two centuries earlier. Both organizations must have played a role in a spiritual breakthrough for Yeats. The influence of these groups on his writing is undeniable. Although we cannot be sure exactly when Yeats started to be fully influenced by either one of the groups, it is noteworthy that the Theosophical Society was founded in 1875 by H. S. Olcott[17] and H. P. Blavatsky. In 1890, the year before she died, Blavatsky is said to have started a closed esoteric section of the Theosophical Society; Yeats was a member of this group too.

Olcott's address *"My Stand for the Theosophical Society,"* a classic in Theosophical circles, puts the overall mission of the group squarely: "if I understand the spirit of this Society, it consecrates itself to the intrepid and conscientious study of truth, and binds itself, individually as collectively, to suffer nothing to stand in the way." The Society is a worldwide organization devoted to the study of ageless wisdom and encompasses the study of various religious traditions as well as philosophy, scientific theories and systematic spiritual practice. The three initial objectives of the Society were paramount to its hundreds of lodges and study groups that meet regularly: "To form a nucleus of the universal brotherhood of humanity, without distinction of race, creed, sex, caste, or color. From the beginning, Theosophy sought to encourage the comparative study of religion, philosophy, and science and to investigate unexplained laws of nature and the powers latent in humanity."[18] Thus we witness in Yeats's writing a real aim to get at truths, to reveal them to his readers, but in somewhat veiled symbolism. There is no surprise that he did this, for Yeats apparently worked hard in metaphysical circles to learn and even to practice magic, so it would be almost unnatural to expect him "to give away" secrets. He is quoted as having told a friend that next to his poetry, "magic was the most important pursuit of his life." [19] As we will see shortly, Yeats makes his readers work a bit to get at veiled messages entrenched in his prose; for the unaware, it is possible to read his essays and miss the mystical connections.

About clairvoyant, mystic Helena Blavatsky who co-founded the Theosophical Society embraced by Yeats volumes have been written, but here it is interesting to relate a small story about her with regard to roses. She is said to have had an occasional awful temper; one such time was while she was in India in the presence of a particularly offensive chauvinist on whose head she made a shower of roses fall.[20]

The Hermetic Order of the Golden Dawn's link to the Rosicrucians of today is not at all clear, but there is apparently a connection if no more than in overlap of membership. The order has always embraced the rose in all its power and beauty and used it one of its symbols. Today the Rosicrucians are less hidden and there seem to be several different groups. One of the groups has built an impressive network supporting numerous publications, home study courses, a park in San Jose California, a Rosicrucian Egyptian Museum and even a Rose-Croix University International offering in-depth courses that expand on aspects of Rosicrucian studies, including the universal laws of nature. The University's purpose is to offer students opportunities for personal development and spiritual growth in a classroom environment under the personal instruction of faculty members who are considered experts in their fields of instruction. Yeats had more than a cursory understanding of the rose as a symbol; he knew its full meaning and connection to cosmic consciousness. Seward's analysis astutely took note of the difference in the tone of Yeat's writings after his initiation.

About the Rosicrucians not a lot was generally known during Yeats time and because several groups exist there is some confusion about which is which. Initially, the organization a great need for secrecy so as to keep its work from becoming adulterated, but enough seeped over the transom that we can be certain that a rose cross symbol was essential in its ceremonies. The initial Rosicrucian manuscripts were said to be first circulated in Germany around 1610; generally the society was begun "to afford mutual aid and encouragement in working out the great problems of life and in searching out the secrets of Nature; to facilitate the study of the system of Philosophy founded upon the Kabalah and the doctrines of Hermes Trismegistus."[21] An authority on the Rosicrucian Order, Paul Foster Case has explained that the name lives on and even flourishes because people are attracted by what they've heard about the Order and what they think they know of the early manifestoes which are actually very short, but not intended to "move gross wits."[22] The Order is often misunderstood but does conceal itself from those who are incompetent. Paul Foster Case reminds us that the Order is not an organized society like the Freemasons and membership is not based on paying entrance fees, making an application or participation in a ceremony. "The Rosicrucian Order is like the old definition of the city of Boston: it is a state of mind. One becomes a Rosicrucian: one does not join the Rosicrucians," according to Case.[23] A contemporary booklet published by the organization today underscores that this is still the case. The group is said to "encourage open minded questioning and self-mastery" and to promote a higher "way of life."[24]

However we make sense of the foundations of the Rosicrucians or of the Hermetic Order of the Golden Dawn, a rose cross is used as a symbol by both fraternities and surely must have provided the essential connection to Yeats's psyche and the metaphysical messages he intended in *The Secret Rose.* First and foremost, the rose has been used as a "sign of silence and secrecy." In his "Brief Study of the Rose Cross Symbol," Thomas D. Worrel explained "the rose, like the cross, has paradoxical meanings." It is at once a symbol of purity and a symbol of passion, heavenly perfection and earthly passion, virginity and fertility, death and life." [25] What's more the rose has significance in numerology. According to Worrel, it represents "the number 5 because it has five petals. And the petals on roses are in multiples of five. Geometrically, the rose corresponds with the pentagram and pentagon."[26] In the Rosicrucian teachings, the "number 5 represents Spirit and the four elements."

But why did the Rosicrucians and other related groups like the Golden Dawn even bother to exist? What was the reason they came on the scene in the first place? Lynn Picknett and Clive Prince in *The Templar Revelation* provide an excellent interpretation of the whys and wherefores of the Order. The Rosicrucian movement and teachings were a major threat to the Catholic Church. The "idea of mankind's essentially **divine** status did not accord with the Christian idea of the 'original sin'—the idea that all men and women are born sinful because of the fall of Adam and Eve." [27] Rosicrusicians of that time went underground, became secret out of necessity not because they wanted to operate in secret per se. The Order was fully established long before the movement was noticed in the seventeenth century; "in fact it is scarcely an exaggeration to say that Rosicrucianism was the Renaissance." [28]

The Golden Dawn embraces both the lotus flower and the rose in its symbols. The Rose Cross Lamen is used prominently in consecration ceremonies and is worn at all meetings of Adepts. This symbol is so sacred to the Order that the instruction is given that it should never to be touched by persons. [29] The Rose Cross of the Order of the Golden Dawn is intricate and magnificently colorful; each part of it has profound meaning, but roses—rings of them—are at the center of the cross and each circle of them has meaning related to the elements, to the ancient seven planets and to the twelve signs of the zodiac and correspondence to the Hebrew alphabet. So the influence on Yeats's *Secret Rose* is clear.

What's more, studying Yeat's short story *Secret Rose* carefully, it is almost impossible not to see parallels to the crucifixion of Jesus Christ, or to even more recently to the tragic death of well known civil rights leader Dr. Martin Luther King, Jr. Both died ultimately, prematurely, in one way or the other—as does the protagonist in *Secret Rose*, for "stirring up the people" toward truth to use a phrase from Yeats. Seekers of truth are generally no strangers to dissociation and dissonance in their connection to nonseekers although it is their aim to connect. The disjunct with others more than likely results from the elevated frequencies that occur when one is seriously on the path of truth and higher awareness.

Yeats published *The Secret Rose* in 1897. Recalling the piece simply, outside of Seward's analysis and in more detail, it is an odd, short piece about an outcast named Cumhal who as a bard was doing what he did best: travel from hamlet to hamlet in a "particoloured doublet" singing and reciting poetry. Known in Ireland of the time as a gleeman, young Cumhal described his own soul as "indeed like the wind, and it blows me to and fro, up and down and puts many things into my mind and out of my mind, and therefore I am called the swift, wild horse."[30] Yeats paints the portrait of Cumhal as an outcast, one who managed late one evening to so offend a certain friar named Coarb that he decided to kill him. The friar's reasoning was clear as to why the poet should be put to death by crucifixion: "the bards and the gleemen are an evil race, ever cursing and ever stirring up the people, and immoral and immoderate in all things, and heathen in their hearts."[31] Obviously, Yeats paints the friar with an inability to see himself: full of mean spirit, hateful and swift to judge as he prepares to complete a bleak, horrific act.

The atrocious friar determined quickly that crucifixion was the appropriate punishment for the gleeman; and so Coarb even managed to awaken fellow monks from their sleep to seek assistance in overseeing the construction of a cross on which to hang the gleeman. Friar Coarb wanted to spread meanness around a bit; it wasn't enough to contain it within himself. But all during the construction of the cross, Cumhal seems undaunted, not fearful, still a free spirit, for he knows something the friar and his accomplices do not know. The gleeman's being is entrusted to the Holy Spirit, as Yeats reveals so subtly in the metaphor of a rose: "...I have been the more alone upon the roads and by the sea, because I heard in my heart the rustling of the rose-bordered dress of her who is ...subtle-hearted and more lovely than a bursting dawn to them that are lost in the darkness."[32] In the foregoing lines, the rose-bordered dress is indeed, metaphorically, the Holy Spirit. Unbeknownst to the friar and his accomplices, Cumhal has already made the intimate connection. Prepared and unafraid to die an earthly death because he knows something profound, Cumhal already has everlasting life.

In his selection of character and plot, Yeats assuredly confronts and affronts an ancient, pervasive problems of the Christian Church and indeed a number of world religions: deceit, violence, hypocrisy and egoism. The friar, showing no mercy, was very quick to judge the gleeman; so quick in fact that he could not wait until morning for fellow clergy to awaken so he could influence them to put Cumhal to death. In one swift, bold move, as Yeats paints him, the friar makes a 180-degree turn about from the real, true teachings of Jesus Christ of the Christian Bible. The friar swiftly steps over of the tenets of the Christian faith: forgiveness, love, charity and tolerance to determine that the young bard should die immediately simply because of ill words toward the Church. Yeats sets up his characters provocatively to make a profound criticism of clergy and, since the monks acted in collusion, the Church itself.

In *The Secret Rose*, Yeats' selection of adjectives such as "swift, wild horse" are pregnant with metaphysical meaning. The gleeman was not afraid to be crucified because he was safely in a connection with the one and only incorporeal God or what those in the metaphysical tradition would refer to as endlessness or cosmic consciousness. Moreover, Yeats describes the gleeman as having a "bulging wallet" another metaphoric indicator that he was full of what Christians commonly refer to as "Holy Spirit." And thus the story goes on to a scene leading up to the crucifixion when Cumhal gives away what is the equivalent of his last supper; the gleeman throws strips of bacon among beggars who fought until the last scrap was eaten. Yeats gives his main character, Cumhal very few last words to moan in the midst of the grumbling beggars before he dies. "Outcasts," he calls to their unheeding ears, "have you turned against outcasts?"

More than six centuries before Yeats, and nearly a century before Dante used the rose in carnal and spiritual symbolic manifestations, Mevlana Jelaluddin Rumi an evolved Afghanistan-born spiritual writer made the same provocative flower an essence in his poetry. Born on September 30th 1207 in Balkh when Afghanistan was still part of the Persian empire, Rumi was instructed by his father's secret inner life and became a sheikh—a religious scholar who helped the poor.[33] But the pivotal event in his life seems to have been meeting the enigmatic saint Shamsi Tabrizi, his teacher and spiritual guide.

As a result of the remarkable translation work of Coleman Barks, Kabir Helminski and others we can now experience Rumi's delightful, spirited poetry firsthand. Barks and his team translate so smoothly that it is almost as if Rumi wrote originally in English. Or is it the case the Rumi's poetry is so spiritually profound, so inspired that the intended messages cannot be missed in translation? For me, the resonance of Rumi's poetry seems to transcend all earthly language. The poems reverberate even in translation although they were not originally written in English. The lines are so pure that they seem palpably connected to Spirit, it seems as if Rumi's poetry was *intended* to be translated and circulated in a variety of global languages. Coleman Barks's collection, *The Essential Rumi* is simply a splendid capturing of Rumi's allegorical and spiritual poetry as it was meant to be. Witness for instance Rumi's "Spring Is Christ." The lines "We walk out to the garden to let the apple meet the peach, to carry messages between rose and jasmine"[34] clearly signify connections between the carnal and spiritual as do the next several lines that use the rose as a metaphor for reaching "a lamp"—of course the lamp is the "Holy Spirit.:"

Spring Is Christ

Raising martyred plants from their shrouds
Their mouths open in gratitude, wanting to
   be kissed.
The glow of the rose and the tulip means a
   lamp
Is inside…[35]

There is more than one use of the rose in Barks's collection, but it is Rumi's *"Dying Laughing"* that seems most poignant in its use of the rose in metaphysical symbolism. The poem opens with a lover who told his beloved how much he loved her and how "faithful and self-sacrificing" he was toward her. "There was fire in him. He didn't know where it came from…"[36] But his beloved was apparently not impressed with all the material things he'd done and she told him as much. She remarked to him in essence that he had done very well as a lover in outwardly acts but he hadn't died. To hear that he had not died struck him as funny since he'd done so very much for his intended.

> When he heard that, he lay back on the ground laughing, and died. He opened like a rose That drops to the ground and died laughing.[37]

It is when the lover died laughing, a metaphor for letting go of the material world that he "opened like a rose" that is to say he made the quantum leap toward cosmic consciousness. The point is that again and again the poet Rumi shows us that he knew and understood everything necessary to make the ultimate connection toward eternal life, long before Dante's epic was written.

Not too far a field from the character Cumhal in Yeat's *Secret Rose* or the lover in Rumi's poem who learned to "die laughing," the old man in Hakim Sanai's poem "*The Old Man of Basra*" lived in a constant struggle to make the connection with the Holy Spirit. The old man arises daily to the same mundane, unessential questions that millions of human beings worldwide ask daily "What shall I eat?" and "What shall I wear?"[38] The old timer lived in constant resistance to such questions when they plagued his psyche. To the question what shall I eat, he learned to answer "death," and to the question, what shall I wear, he learned to answer "a winding sheet." These answers revealed spiritual evolvement; the old man of Basra was fighting to overcome the material world. Sanai, writing nearly a hundred years before Rumi, used "garden roses" oddly, in juxtaposition, to show that for "self-Cherishers" roses assume the form of "malignant boils." This is the case for those who are imprisoned by the three prisons of "deceit, hatred and envy" reminiscent of the three beasts encountered by Dante in the *Divine Comedy*. Sanai, about whom little is known, lived during the reign of Bahramshah

(1118–1152) and probably died in 1150.[39] His work is little known in the West, but has a deeply metaphysical quality to it.

Thus, not only Rumi but Sanai knew eons before Dante and Yeats precisely what the latter came to know as a result of deep study of the ancient teachings. Connection to the Light of the Source takes study and work, a lot of it, that is done in gradations. Dante Alighieri was guided by allegorical messages in St. Jerome's Latin Vulgate version of *The Holy Bible* that he likely studied and mastered. In his epic poem, he astutely uses Beatrice as a guide; she had rebuffed him in real life. Thus, in an interesting juxtaposition, Alighieri shows that he has overcome the material world. Yeats, in his association with the Theosophical Society and the Order of the Golden Dawn, we can be sure is likely to have had teachers or guides to hermetic knowledge; Helena Blavatsky was surely one of them. Yeats in his connection to several esoteric organizations had many opportunities to become privy to hidden knowledge that has been kept out of the reach the profane masses. He was fully involved in metaphysical studies and had reached a high level of understanding about realms that are far beyond the material world. It has been said that when the student is ready, a teacher will appear. For Rumi, Tabrizi arrived when he was ready; for Sanai we can't be sure since he lived so long ago and not much has been written about him, but it appears that his teachers were Lai-Khur and Yusuf Hamadani.[40]

One has only to look at the meanness and lack of humility in the world today to understand why mystics and adepts were careful not to waste time on "gross wits" and on those who refused to do the necessary work toward what mystically based secret societies refer to as "self mastery."[41] What all of these great writers and poets from Yeats to Rumi apparently knew well is that human beings are supposed to mimic the rose in their behavior in order to trump the material world. Other essays in this collection follow the trail of the rose in its connection to a *shift* in consciousness.

Chapter Two

Rose Vignettes:
Black Plague to Gulag

In 1938, German-Jewish poet and writer Rudolf Borchardt published one of his last works, a masterpiece of a book under the title *The Passionate Gardner*. In this little known work of about 340 pages that has been translated to English by Henry Martin, Borchardt uses plants and gardening as a deep antecedent for the potentiality of human beings to grow up, to master themselves and to create something good for all of mankind. Borchardt beseeches us to understand a "grandiose metaphor in which the human soul is itself a garden, strictly and fervently in the care of God: the heart of the child of the world is rife with weeds, and He plucks them up; the heart of the innocent is a pious modest field full of silent grace, and fragrant with fine perfume…"[42]

It is no coincidence that various versions the *Holy Bible* of the Christian tradition open with the scene of a garden. Borchardt reminds his readers cogently that the scene in which Christ took his pained departure from the world also took place in the garden of Gethsemane. Thus, "purity can only be found within the protection of vegetation and everything which is not impure is a garden." The garden then ultimately is a place of order, where man is potentially master and transformer. Borchardt used the garden and flowers as a metaphor for the great work that human beings can accomplish when they are able to transcend the ordinary, to open up, to bloom like so many flowers. By this view, there is significant merit in pure work that leads to creation of something good for all of human kind. Constance Casey, who reviewed **The Passionate Gardner** for the **New York Times** in 2006, refers to Borchardt's work as a form of "botanical globalism" that points us to the heart of an urgent matter in gardening: "whether to grow native plants only, or to permit plants from other continents in our gardens." Ultimately gardeners can make the choice of whether to reach out to embrace plants that are uncommon to the area or to settle for provincialism—that is to stay with plants and choices that are common to their geographic areas.

This metaphor from gardening is easily applied to service to humanity. Are we to live separately, selfishly and just for our own families and immediate circles or do we swing outside that realm to create something wonderful and transcendent for the good of all? In this regard, it is important to underscore the fact that the rose lends itself to cross breeding more than any other flower and also renders a number of gifts to humans, including beauty, medicinal qualities, fragrance and perfection in its very essence. In this sense, the rose serves humanity as something beautiful and useful. The choice of staying comfortably within our own spheres or swinging out of the familiar to connect with, to help, and to support others and to make a difference through creating something wonderful that all can benefit from is available to all of us. A number of great human beings have understood Borchardt's powerful metaphor of botanical globalism and have reached far beyond themselves, often through great adversity, to create something good, beautiful and useful that advances or aids human beings. This is the acid test, to move away from our own trials and tribulations to do something for others: to work intently, to serve others for no gain to ourselves, no matter what the adversities. Very difficult work indeed; some of us cannot even understand why it is paramount.

Borchardt's powerful insights and metaphors of gardens and flowers point us poignantly to individuals who have embraced the rose in a number of manifestations, including healing, music, social justice and world peace for the rose is quite singularly a symbolic presence in all of these. When it comes to metaspiritual matters, the rose is a remarkably useful symbol of the opening of the chakras, those urgent, unseen energy centers in the human body that average human beings never come to know. When we consider the vastness and universality of the rose, the flower no doubt reaches its earthly paragon or highest level when Daniel Andreev put it forth as a potent symbol of all people uniting in one deeply moral force for world peace. We will meet Andreev in this chapter and others like him who have known the superior qualities of the rose in their work, often as a result of a strong spiritual connection or light that revealed itself quite vibrantly when one is ready.

The extraordinary beings who have understood the utter necessity for work that aids others and so eludes most of us have traversed this earth in diverse geographic locations in practically all epochs and have made their marks in most legendary, extraordinary ways as will be explored in this essay. Given the focus of these essays, who would be surprised to know that the work of these individuals in some way embraced the rose, not only symbolically, but also practically since the botanical essence of various roses has been found to possess magnificent medicinal qualities.

Dr. Edward Bach

So let us consider healing and medicinal properties of the rose first as understood and used by Dr. Edward Bach (1886–1936). Bach, a British physician who studied medicine at the University College Hospital, London, found plants as a curative after abandoning his traditional, successful practice. Bach's work with plants was antithetical to the traditional Western approach to medicine. He is said to have come to the understanding of plant essences psychically. The flowers used by Bach are thought to be "higher order" since they contain frequencies that are within the human energy field.[43] This is perhaps a novel idea for most of us who have never considered flowers to be more than lovely to look at, sometimes to smell or to adorn tables and parlors. The human soul is thought to contain 38 qualities or virtues that are the same qualities of flowers selected by or "given to" Dr. Bach from a higher realm. The energy or divine sparks of these flowers are like wavelengths in the energy field that Bach came to know intuitively.[44] Dr. Bach introduced the essence of wildflower blooms, including rock rose and wild rose to treat all sorts of ailments, including asthma, irritable bowel syndrome, headaches, muscular tension, rashes and more. Bach flower essences, a spin off of the ideas of homoeopathy but said to be more pure because they lack the products of the disease, are now carried in top health food stores world wide and are also available through mail order. The essences can also be used to treat mental upsets such as remorse or lack of confidence. Based on these 38 powerful flower essences, Dr. Bach's work is also akin to herbal medicine, but has as its foundation his thought that "disease is in essence the result of conflict between Soul and Mind."[45] Bach reminds us that although bacteria plays a part in the spread of physical disease, it is only part of the equation because not everyone exposed to bacteria gets sick or develops disease; there are factors higher than the material world that must be considered.[46] In his essay "*Heal Thyself*," Bach explained that disease serves the purpose of letting us know our essential faults and if we can correct the fault, the disease has been beneficial and will be alleviated:

> No effort directed to the body alone can do more than superficially repair damage, and in this there is no cure, since the cause is still operative and may at any moment again demonstrate its presence in another form. In fact, in many cases apparent recovery is harmful, since it hides from the patient the true cause of his trouble, and in the satisfaction of apparently renewed health the real factor, being unnoticed, may gain strength.

Throughout recorded history, a few extraordinary people like Edward Bach have mastered themselves and the feat of connecting with others for the purpose of advancing work that aids humanity. Ironically, as we are beginning to see, all of these individuals from countries and cultures wide and far have in some way used or embraced the rose in their work.

Nostradamus, 16th Century France

Although there were detractors and disbelievers all around him, the great Michael de Nostradamus led an extraordinary life and his powers seemed to increase as the years progressed. From the universe, Nostradamus was given the unusual, bitter-sweet gift of prophecy. His work and predictions have not gone unnoticed in the past five hundred years for a number of films, books and articles have chronicled his life and work. More than an astute physician, clairvoyant and mage, the Frenchman known simply as Nostradamus predicted the explosion at the World Trade Center in New York and numerous other devastating events over past centuries. Destined to be as controversial as he was sought after for his psychic powers by the rich and the royal, Nostradamus was conversely thought by his wife's family to be a failure for his inability to save his own family from the Black plague when it struck Agen in southern France of 1537. For this failure, he was asked to return the dowry paid by his wife's family at the time of their marriage. An Italian doctor and apparently jealous friend, Julius-Cesar Scaliger (1484–1580), provoked a bitter quarrel between Nostradamus and his in-laws which shattered their friendship; this hurtful time was followed by a charge of heresy and exile from Agen.

Ian Wilson's fine biography of Nostradamus provides an excellent translation from the treasurer of Aix-en-Provence when the plague hit that town in 1546, less than a decade after it struck Nostradamus's family. Victims suffered greatly: "Black egg-sized swellings or buboes would appear in the armpits and groin, oozing blood and pus. Black blotches would follow all over the skin accompanied by severe pain and within five days the victim would usually be dead."

Although there was said to be no known cause and no known cure, the conditions ushering in the plague were a combination of strange weather patterns and unsanitary living habits that left Europe ripe for an epidemic of some sort. Peter Lemesurier, a Cambridge-trained linguist and teacher has helped us to put the foundation causes of the plague in perspective. By the 1520's, Lemesurier explains how the conditions for the plague started while "Europe's Little Ice Age was in full swing. As a result winters were tending to become more artic, summers colder and wetter. Even when plowing and sowing could be done at all, the crops would often rot in the fields. No crops meant no food, and no food meant no survival."[47] As a result of this strange weather pattern, France suffered agriculturally and experienced "no fewer than thirteen major famines during the course of the century."

But Europe also suffered flooding as a result of strange weather patterns. It is clear that odd weather patterns aided and abetted flooding and that coupled with trauma to the agricultural system was a mix for disaster. By 1544, heavy rains caused the Rhone River to rise beyond normal levels causing flooding of towns and cemeteries; corpses washed out of their graves and exceptionally awful sanitation problems led to the plague.[48]

Although the predictions of Nostradamus and even his life's story have been well recorded, information about his clever use of rose petals in a mixture as a preventative during the years of the plague is scant. Ian Wilson interprets and recounts Nostradamus's own *Treatise on cosmetics and jams* that prescribes use of the rose as a preventive for those who had not yet caught the plague.

> Take some sawdust or shavings of cypress-
> wood, as green as you can find, one ounce;
> iris of Florence, six ounces; cloves, three
> ounces; sweet calamus [cane palm], three

drams; aloes-wood six drams. Grind everything to powder and take care to keep it all
airtight. Next take some furled red roses,
three or four hundred, clean, fresh and
culed before dewfall. Crush them to powder
in a marble mortar, wooden pestle.

Nostradamus then advised adding more half-unfurled
roses to the mixture and rose juice as well. He advised further
that the mixture should be made into pill form and that it
would smell good too. What the great mage did not explain
and may not have known in the scientific-medical language
of his time is that rose petals contain important phytochem-
icals such as beta-carotene, betulin, catchechin, flavonoids
and nutrients such as calcium, iron, magnesium, manganese,
phosophorus and potassium; the petals also contain an array
of B vitamins and is generally good for infections of all kinds.

Dr. Tomin Harada, World War II Era, Japan

Few in America or Europe outside of medical profession
have heard of Tomin Harada, for before World War II he was

just another professional serving his country as he was trained and expected to do as a military physician. The World War II era changed all of that. Born in 1912, Harada graduated from Jikei Medical School in Tokyo in 1936 and soon after in 1938 was trust into war with China, one of the opening stages of World War II. Dr. Harada put himself in a tense situation as a military officer-surgeon when he was asked to talk to a group of soldiers using a canned model prepared for him for such occasions. "…I just could not bring myself to pass on such nonsense." So Harada decided to speak from his heart and remembered his speech to be something like this:

> Although the Japanese and Chinese races
> are slightly different, we along
> With the Tungas people, the Koreans, and
> the Melanesians, all have Chinese
> Blood flowing in our veins. More impor-
> tantly, Japan has received much from
> Chinese culture. We are now fighting, but
> we must not let this become a war
> Of hatred. The time will surely come when
> we will be friends again. We are going

now to help create an opportunity for
that friendship to be reawakened.

Given his officer training, Harada was embarrassed by
the speech later after thought about what he'd said. Harada
had not been able to bring himself to say purely military
inspired things that he didn't believe. Harada was critical of
Japan's notion that it should rule the world just as he resented
the colonialism of Great Britian, the United States and
Holland. Stationed at the Taiwan's Henchun garrison amid
poisonous snakes and mountain leeches, Harada, then practically emaciated from the long campaign with few rations left,
remembered the day the news came that the war was over.
He also found out shockingly that Hiroshima and Nagasaki
had been attached by Atomic bombs. Eventually returning to
his hometown of Hiroshima, he found it obliterated and his
family missing. With the aid of a friend who survived, Harada
eventually found his family at their ancestral home outside of
town and soon after set himself to work building a hospital in
1946 to help the survivors of the bomb's devastating impact.

It was after the war and the death of his wife that Harada
became a passionate peace activist and in retirement pro-

moted growing roses in connection with peace activism. He met another former WWII officer in the UK who introduced him to roses. Harada immediately took to the lovely, fragrant flower and became a breeder; both men agreed that roses could be used as a symbol of world peace. It is noteworthy that two former officers who had seen the horrors of war from opposing sides could now embrace the simple, fragrant rose as a symbol of world peace.

Dr. Harada's superior reconstructive, plastic surgery in the treatment of the bombing victims in Japan and later his treatment also of those who suffered maladies of the herbicide agent orange and napalm used in the Viet Nam War were progressive and legendary. He is said to have been especially attracted to roses because the fresh flower reminded him of the young and beautiful children who had been killed in the war and would never have the opportunity to lead the world toward peace. In crossbreeding roses, Dr. Harada developed new brands that he gave unusual names such as "Phoenix Hiroshima, Hiroshima Mind, Miss Hiroshima, Peace Maker, Red Hiroshima, Dr. Tomin, May Peace, Spirit Hiroshima…" and so on that still exist in Hiroshima and in select gardens all over Japan.[49] During his life time, Dr. Harada attempted to send some of the flowers he bred to world leaders with the wish for no more nuclear war and a "free" world. Dr. Harada explained, "Let the roses speak for themselves. Roses embody peace and beauty by themselves." His rose initiative caught on in the corridors of Japan and perhaps the peace movement in that country today is a spin off of his untiring work with roses for peace. He died in June 1999.

Mozart (1756–1791), Austria

The rose is a powerful symbolic presence in the universe, but its connection to semiotics is easy to miss for the profane and noisy probably because the flower itself is at once quiet, beautiful and refined. Likewise high vibration beautiful music seems rarely to be enjoyed by the profane. Song writers and composers all over the globe have embraced the rose in exquisite compositions and it could be deduced from a couple of striking examples that at least some of those who have used the flower were no strangers to higher awareness. This is certainly the case with Mozart. When his life and work are carefully studied, it is apparent that he knew a lot about higher awareness and mysticism and there may have been resentment from colleagues that he revealed it. Thus speculation continues that breaking silence about secrets revealed to him in Masonic initiation may have led to his mysterious, untimely death. Wolfgang Amadeus Mozart as a child prodigy mastered the violin, harpsichord and organ and went on to compose some of the greatest classical music of all times. The evidence is that Mozart during this short life knew the mystic rose. One of his greatest renditions, *Die Zauberflote* or *Magic Flute* mostly finished between 1790–91 just before he died, speaks volumes about arcane messages of the rose. The opera was written to convey important Masonic and mystical messages, although that fact is apparently grasped by only a few who have seen and heard the opera world wide. Naturally, the rose adumbrates in this most widely known work, one that is rift with secret symbols. Important tenets of Freemasonry are service, silence, patience, steadfastness: these are replete in the *Magic Flute*. It is not by chance that Judy Taymor's breathtaking production of the *Magic Flute* at New York City's Metropolitan Opera during the 2007–2008 seasons prominently depicts a rose garden in act two, scene three. Taymor, an award winning, renowned theatrical producer, was so astute as to make the roses lighted, crystal, red and colossal in size. The rose symbolizes love, discretion, and the potential for connection with the Source of all and everything; it is truly the mystic rose. Both the garden and the rose are potent symbols that can lead to the light of Cosmic Consciousness—that is to say to becoming one with the Source, for those who are aware and not blinded by deceit, ego, and greed. This truth has been veiled for hundreds of years while various denominational divides were purposely created to keep the masses better managed, manipulated and placated.

In *The Magic Flute*, protagonists Pamina and Tamino, lovers in the opera, overcome evil in their midst and grow tremendously in their understanding that true love is unconditional and never too possessive. These are most difficult lessons for Pamina who does not comprehend Tramino's silence during his initiation to higher consciousness. She lacks Tamino's discipline and resolve to stay the course, to become a master, first and foremost of himself. With the aid of three spirits, Pamina eventually finds Tamino and walks with him through many ordeals symbolized in the opera by trials connected with water and fire. Through it all they are protected by a magic flute. They are united in marriage at the end of the opera, but this too is a very, most powerful and misunder-stood symbol in mysticism.

Now this marriage that takes place between Pamina and Tamino in *The Magic Flute* is important to consider closely for it teaches us much about the real meaning of marriage as it is practiced worldwide. "Marriage and intercourse, whether legal or illicit, refer not to any carnal relationship but to a spiritual "marriage", or blending of consciousness, at any level.[50] Thus, as we come to understand that the practice of marriage on earth is really symbolic of the potential of the human being to rise up, to fuse with the light that transcends darkness. The ultimate goal always is to connect with and become one with Cosmic Consciousness. When individuals marry, a fusion or uniting is supposed to take place such that the two rise up to become more than each one could have been solo, but often that does not occur in our troubled world. This knowledge that marriage is intended to *symbolize* all that is sacred is urgent and important for us involved in the ultimate earthly relationship of matrimony to keep in mind. Most of us have not been socialized to understand what the institution of marriage truly signifies, but the troubled practice continues world wide. Even when the truth of the institution of marriage has been made available in metaphor and symbols such as the rose and the cross, human beings still do not get it: intense work on the part of both partners is involved to make successful marriages on earth and likewise intense work is necessary to reach the light of the Holy Spirit. Rather than doing the intense work, the preference of human beings has been to intellectualize the real messages provided in scripture through talk. Egos abound too and get in the way of successful marriages on earth; it goes without saying that too much ego is a impediment to connection to Cosmic realms just as it impedes successful relationships in our daily lives. Commitment to the work associated with rising up has to be great, so much so that most human beings cannot or will not discipline themselves to perform it. Likewise the institution of marriage, like sex between a man and a woman, are simply not routine matters. Inherent in these earthly relationships of sex and marriage is the truth that we as human beings all are intended to connect with each other, to love and to be supportive to one another and ultimately to connect with the Source of us all. We are not on earth to war with each other. We may never understand this essential truth. Great efforts have been made to block it from our understanding.

Charles Austin Miles, New Jersey, USA

Little is known about American Charles Austin Miles (1868–1946) at this remove. Most people today have never even heard his name uttered but practically all in the protestant Christian tradition know his song "In the Garden" as a staple of Sunday church services. The song was "given" to Miles in 1912 as a result of a request for him to write a hymn text that would be "sympathetic in tone, breathing tenderness in every line; one that would bring hope to the hopeless, rest for the weary, and downy pillows to dying beds."[51] Miles was guided in writing the song by a vision of Jesus preceded by opening his Bible to John 20, the meeting of Jesus and Mary. Seated in a dark room at the time, Miles' account of writing the famous song has been described in *101 Hymn Stories* just as he remembered it:

> I awakened in full light, gripping the Bible, with muscles tense and nerves vibrating. Under the inspiration of this vision I wrote as quickly as the words could be formed the

poem exactly as has since appeared. That same evening I wrote the music.

Like the writer William Butler Yeats whose work embracing the rose was discussed in the last Chapter, Charles Austin Miles had Masonic connections as mentioned in his 1946 obituary in the *New York Times*.[52] Miles was born in Lakehurst, New Jersey and was the author of 3,000 hymns. *"In the Garden"* was not considered a financial success in Miles's lifetime, although it sold three million copies and recordings exceeded one million. The hymn has worldwide distribution and is sung in many languages.[53] We can only speculate that he have been a member of one of the secret societies such as the Rosicrucians or even the Order of the Golden Dawn since both fraternities embrace the rose fully. Miles was precise in his lyrics embracing roses in a garden for the composition of *"In the Garden."* The dew on the roses Miles refers to is symbolic of light. Obviously, Miles knew something about Cosmic Consciousness; he had apparently tapped it based on his description of how the song was "given" to him.

I come to the garden alone

While the dew is still on the roses

And the voice I hear falling on my ear

The song of God discloses

In biblical hidden teachings, a garden is symbolic of paradise and by now it is essential that we also know that the red rose when fully opened symbolizes connection of the key crown charka to what has been synomously called cosmic consciousness, the universal mind, Christ consciousness or God. It is also clear that each of us must make the journey to the Source alone, thus the opening line of the song, "I come to the garden alone."

Daniel Andreev

In his own realm—that is to say the mid-twentieth century metaphysical community in Soviet Russia, Daniel Andreeve was the mastermind of an incredible work known simply as **The Rose of the World**. At the time that he wrote the masterpiece, no one in the West knew of it and very few in Russia knew of the work either because by 1947 Daniel

Andreev had been sentenced to 25 years in a gulag for his outspoken ideas and other writings that were considered anti-Soviet. Andreev's pre-gulag work was destroyed; his opus **The Rose of the World** was written while he was in prison, hidden with the aid of those around him who thought the work worthwhile, buried until the collapse of the Soviet system, printed first in Russian in Moscow and now in English. And no wonder the harsh Soviet system repressed Andreev and his work. No words were minced about the evils of power hungry government officials by Andreev in **The Rose of the World**. He gets to the heart of heady political and economic matters that beg to be confronted by citizens all over the globe, now more than ever. In recent English translation by Jordan Roberts, Andreev's writings proffer the notion that human beings should be tremendously concerned about the formation of a global police state that he felt was in the making. Andreev's vision was that new technological advances simply helped along the process of a global police state. Andreev wrote sometime between 1947 and 1957:

> *It should come as no surprise today that one side of every scientific and technical*

advance goes against the genuine interests of humanity.

The internal combustion engine, radio, aviation, atomic energy—they all strike the bare flesh of the world's people with one end, while advances in communications and technology enable police states to establish surveillance over the private life and thoughts of each person thus laying an iron foundation for life-sucking dictatorial states.

It is eerie to recall Andreev's warnings now, more than fifty years later, considering American writer Norman Mailer's pronouncement just before he died in 2007 that the devil's principal weapon is technology. Mailer seemed to believe that the devil aspires to create a mechanized world where "souls are increasingly interchangeable." Whether that's true or not, we can see evidence now, and it does seem clear that technology often hurts as much as it helps sort of like the Southern story of the cow who gives a splendid bucket of milk and then takes her hind leg and kicks it over. Human beings are too much steeped in usage of cell phones, computers, ipods and such to even notice or care that these are used as potent tracking devices that are an invasion of privacy. The breech of quiet and safety for others caused by impolite cell phone use is out of control. Coupled with high tech weapons, all of this so called "technology" is clearly detrimental to all of us now and will be even more so in the long run when radiation is factored. Keen note must be taken of Andreev's admonishments about negative aspects of technology in light of recent televised Congressional hearings on the development of a new mercenary, security force known as Blackwater, USA. This organization and others like it are apparently extraordinary groups of super charged, highly trained men with the latest high tech weapons and technical know how who will go anywhere and do practically anything at the bidding of government.[54]

Andreev was released early from prison after a decade of poor diet, beatings and harsh, cruel treatment that left him broken and very sick. Upon release, an emaciated Andreev knew that his days were numbered, yet he persevered to finish *Rose of the World* which he did just before his death. We are reminded by Mikhail Epstein who has translated and interpreted a large portion of Andreev's work that he was preoccupied with nature and this component drives much of the philosophical underpinning of his work. Epstein concluded:

Throughout his creative years, Daniil Andreev suffered under the

Pressure of official Soviet ideology's "stubborn iron materialism," but

His inner resistance to this mysticism of materiia did not push him to

The other extreme of bodiless spiritualism. Nature was the center of his

Whole system, and he singled out a special category of "elementals" (*stikhiali*), spiritual entities that have an elevating effect on the human

Soul and are embodied in such natural elements (*stikhii*) as rivers, trees, wind, and snow. Daniil Andreev enjoyed traveling through the wildest and most remote Russian forests, because for him nature suggested the most genuine way of knowing God...

His marriage to Alla survived the gulag, but he didn't survive very long after release. Alla Andreeva had suffered too because she was incarcerated in the same system, although at a different locations and away from her husband. Alla Andreeva remembered her time in the gulag as demeaning and harsh. The gulag system was apparently engineered to strip every ounce of individuality and dignity. Ann Applebaum's award winning book *Gulag*, refers to Alla as Anna Andreev and provides much insight into the horrors of the Soviet prison system. At first Mrs. Andreev was sent to a camp where prisoners were allowed to wear their own clothes, but beginning in 1948 she was made to wear a smock dress that she found particularly offensive.[55]

In order to counter the potential for a global government and attendant global police force that he felt were coming, Andreev advocated the necessity for a strong moral body. In **Rose of the World** seems almost to Andreev plead that:

> We must…recognize the absolute necessity
> of the one and only path:
> The establishment, over a global federation
> of states, of an unsullied, incorrupt-
> ible, highly respected body, a moral
> body standing outside of and above the

state. For the state is, by its very nature, amoral.

The Global Anti-FGM Movement

Surely Alice Walker, Pulitzer Prize winning America author, did not anticipate being so roundly criticized and in some corridors practically skewered for her work that brought the horrific practice of female genital mutilation to the spotlight. Since disclosure is essential to the developing global movement to fight female genital mutilation, Walker's book *Possessing the Secret of Joy* was a bit of a blockbuster. After social activist, humanitarian, nurse Efua Dorkenoo read Walker's book, she immediately contacted Walker as she explained to colleague in the struggle Tobe Levin: "I wrote to Alice. You see FORWARD [the organization founded by Dorkenoo to fight the practice] counsels women like Tashi [the main character Walker's book] whose mental anguish at having suffered mutilation has become unbearable. Tashi is so real that I wanted to let Alice know and invite her to be patron of FORWARD. Of course, she agreed..." a FORWARD board meeting in June 1995 specifically credited Alice Walker's work in the long struggle to eradicate the practice. The film *Warrior Marks* was largely inspired and guided by African activists of Efua Dorkenoo's stature but Walker naturally received the lion's share of flack. After the film was shown in London, Dorkenoo even received death threats since she was a promoter of the film, an avid fighter against FGM and now lives in the UK. Walker continues to be criticized. In 1993, *Newsweek* quoted Dr. Nahid Toubia who said Alice Walker was a "writer whose star is fading... trying to sensationalize in order to get the limelight back." Equally alarming, in a 1993 New York Times editorial, African residents of the United States blamed Walker for their distress, reducing to personal display her attention to "their" issue. Despite an abundance of criticism, Walker, like Dorkenoo, has courageously continued her work and both have been propelled, not quieted.

Efua Dorkenoo, OBE, is a brilliant nurse and native of Ghana who moved to the UK in the 1970s and is one of the earliest campaigners against FGM. She founded FORWARD (Foundation for Women's Health Research and Development) in London in 1983, presently the largest, oldest and among the most respected NGO's outside of Africa. Dorkenoo's organization has inspired similar groups in Germany (founded in

1998), Nigeria (1999) and Somalia (2005). She has testified before the United States Congress about the magnitude of the practice of FGM and is a recipient of an award and monetary grant from the British government in light of her work, founded FORWARD in the UK to heat up the fight. Who better to tell the story of the horrors of FGM than a top notch nurse and former mid-wife who has seen the health risks, inflection and death associated with the practice? Naturally, because the guarded practice is so well entrenched in Africa and parts of the Middle East, Dorkenoo continues to take a lot of heat for her work. But she was able to reach Senator Edward Kennedy propelling him into the forefront of international advocacy against FGM. She also inspired congresswomen Patricia Schroeder and Barbara Rose Collin's toward House Resolution 3247 against FGM in the United States. There have been many other highlights to Dorkenoo's courageous work, but the Human Rights Award she received from feminist organization Equality Now, founded in 1992 was a big deal to her. In 2005, Dorkenoo received the coveted award from hands of actress Meryl Streep at a ceremony in New York. It is Dorkenoo's book *Cutting the Rose: Female Genital Mutilation, the Practice and Its Prevention* that offers up the rose as the centerpiece symbol of the developing global movement against FGM. The rose of course symbolizes the coveted, sacred, powerful vagina and FGM involves the practices of *infibulation*, the sewing closed of the vaginal opening and *clitoridectomy*, the removal of the clitoris, both horrifying to think about. What's more, a league of Nigerian artists, including men like Godfrey Williams-Okorodus who resides in Antwerp, Belgium, have used the rose in various ways in their paintings and art work to aid in the fight against FGM. Okorodus's art work is part of an international traveling exhibition of watercolor and oil works that address the horrors of FGM.

Following the first edition of **Cutting the Rose**, Dorkenoo accomplished another pioneering feat: in July 1992, as the head of FORWARD-UK, she organized the First Study Conference on FGM in the European Diaspora which took place in London and served as the forerunner to intensive European organizing, culminating in the European Network against Harmful Traditional Practices (EuroNet FGM) founded in Brussels in 2002.

Tobe Levin, collegiate professor in the University System of Maryland in Europe lives in Germany, came to the anti-

FGM movement in 1977 after reading a magazine article that galvanized her, appropriate for her profession since she teaches literature. The magazine was *EMMA*, a German feminist publication and the article was *"Klitorisbeschneidung"* (clitoridectomy) written by journalist Pauline Caravello. Levin couldn't believe what she was reading, "They do what?!!" was her immediate reaction. What she felt at once was empathy and rage. Levin, an avid social activist and now a publisher of anti-FGM related books, well remembers the day she read the article and the magazine's stillness as she stared at what she'd read with fugitive shrieks that bounced off the walls. Levin also recalls that just thinking about the contents of the article caused her to dive under her duvet with legs crossed, tight. Levin, who is a wife and mother, could not believe that so many women in countries throughout Africa and the Middle East were denied the right to make decisions about their bodies. The FGM practice is so culturally entrenched that often elder women are the chief perpetuators and promoters. Levin vowed to do something and she has for thirty years running. Immediately after reading the article in *EMMA*, Levin contacted the only African campaigners against FGM that she could find: Awa Thiam, Edna Adan Ismail, Nawal el Saadawi and Marie Assaad. With an abundance of continued criticism, all of them have worked tirelessly to educate people about the practice and to garner support to put a stop to it. It is seemingly lifetime work; the practice is quiet and underground except when young women end up at hospitals or clinics with inflections or worse. It has now more than seeped into the diaspora throughout Europe and the United States with hundreds and hundreds of cases ending up in the medical system. Using the work of Alice Walker and others, Levin routinely educates her students about FGM. She is a co-founder of FORWARD-Germany, companion organization to Efua Dorkenoo's group in the UK.

The women and men who fight against FGM are at all times confronted with the question: How to approach an issue viewed as urgent by only a tiny trans-national minority that is supported with tenacity by an enormous, and excessively powerful majority? It is so incredibly entrenched that as late as 2007 there is proof that the practice was actually done as a way to buy votes in Sierre Leone where 90% of females are said to be cut. One must get graphic about the horrors of the FGM practice in order to confront it. Sadly, FGM has defenders, females at that. In 1991, FORWARD board member and mid-wife

Comfort Ottah confronted defenders in a letter to the editor of *Emerge Magazine,* George Curry. Ottah thinks it is ridiculous to compare male circumcision with FGM and challenged notions by Harriet Washington who as quoted sought to normalize the practice in the **Emerge** article by asking if it's known how many men "go out to satisfy their sexual needs because it is impossible to do so with their wives? Does she know how many women are abandoned by their husbands because they shrink away due to pain each time the husbands come near them for sexual relationship?" Ottah pointed to the number of school girls who stay home from school because they cannot menstruate freely and the number who might spend 30–45 minutes trying to pass urine and are in trouble with their teachers for being late to classes? Comfort Ottah's piercing letter to the editor explained other inconveniences of FGM such as urinary tract infections and worse, a number of deaths of unborn infants is associated with the practice. Finally, Ottah compared FGM to practices like binding of women's feet, chastity belts, denying voting rights to women, slavery and so on, all efforts to oppress or control. "Enough is enough," she concluded.

A fiery voice in the anti-FGM movement is Awa Thiam, one of the women who promoted the film *Warrior Marks* in

London. Born in Senegal, Thiam's best known book is **La Parole aux negresses** (1978). Thiam slams a number of practices that are oppressive of African women, including FGM, polygamy and skin whitening. But Thiam doesn't blame African men solely for these practices. In her book **Black Sisters, Speak Out,** Thiam reminds us that African women also keep alive practices that are oppressive of females. African men, she proffers, were pushed into brutalizing women because white colonialists had made them feel so inferior.

No other flower in the universe is as associated with the unusual talent of select humans as the rose. The talents and insight we have witnessed in this essay run the gamut from medicine and humanitarianism to the pure genius of creating something wonderful like beautiful, timeless music or opera and literature. Apparently human beings were intended to shadow the rose and can fully when they step into the light of service to others or when something beautiful and beneficial is created for the benefit of all.

Chapter Three

"...Blossom As the Rose" in *OAHSPE, The Emerald Tablets,* and *The Holy Bible*

The wilderness and the solitary place shall be Glad for them; and the desert shall rejoice, and Blossom as the rose.

The Holy Bible, (King James Version)
Isaiah 35, Verse 1

In obedience to the law, the word of the Master Grew into flower.

The Emerald Tablets

By his command shall a rose bloom in our
midst.

Book of Saphah, OASPHE

According to an expert on cultural icons and symbolism, the rose is said to hold a "royal status among flowers" explained by "its association with comfort, generosity and discretion.[56] But it is apparently not well known that high level entities in nature and in the universe have been connected to the rose. Inextricable, for instance, is the connection of the rose to the sun, to symbolism of the mystic Jesus Christ who was known as the "rose child" and to the floral symbol of the female vulva.[57] Even the magnificent scent of the flower has been revered by both pagans and patricians over epochs and across global timelines. Donald Tyson's compilation on the history of occult philosophy reminds readers that in every good matter such as love and good will, "there must be good fume, odoriferous and precious" and likewise wherever something bad or at least of no good value is brewing, there are "stinking fumes that are of no worth." During ancient times, the essence of the rose was mixed with all sorts of concoctions including with "musk, red coral, ambergris" and even with unmentionable animal parts to create "suffu-migation," according to the foundations of western occultism. [58] In modern times, the precious oil essence of rose petals has been mixed with numerous other scents to create sought after fragrances that have brought fortunes to the global perfume industry.

While the rose has been well recognized for its ostensible natural qualities and has been used as a diverse symbol globally, mystical aspects of the flower have been the least known and apparently, for most, unknowable. Nevertheless, a bevy of clues and hints about arcane aspects have been given to mankind such as the rose's enticing scent and, more than any other flower, its readiness to be crossbred. Rose petals are smooth, fragrant and could not be more perfect. A most unusual clue about the rose's special mystical place in the universe is symbolized in the fabulously colorful rose nebula mentioned earlier in the introduction of this collection. This giant cosmic nebula spans 50 light years and lies hovering in the cosmos 4,500 light years away from earth, near the constellation Monoceros. [59] Yet few human beings have taken note of its presence probably because it can be seen only with the aid of a powerful telescope. Of the myriad shapes this provocative nebula might have taken, the rose became the resonant form in both magnificent red color and shape. It has been suggested by websites that the nebula's presence was foretold eons ago but no one knows for sure just how long this giant collection of star dust has been in the cosmos. The point of bringing the nebula to mind here is that the rose symbolically and botanically pops up throughout the universe in a variety of ways to render its message for those who have "eyes to see" so to say. The rose has quite a remarkable presence for those who have arrived at higher awareness; it has been taken note of for hundreds and hundreds of years by those who are paying attention to one of the most important, archetypical symbols nature has ever rendered. It should be emphasized again that appearances of the rose or its likeness in the cosmos and in varied sacred literature bespeak the flower's pedagogic role. It is truly the flower of perfection and love, an apropos symbol for the global village. The mission of the rose transcends any particular religion or belief system and over time has been connected to Isis, Aphrodite, Venus, Mary, the Knights Templar, the Rosicrucians, the Order of the Golden Dawn and even to Zen.[60] Alchemists are said to have embraced it as "the flower of knowing" or "rosarium philosophorum." Its message is irrespective of religion; those who are mired in the dogma of any political or religious persuasion are the most unlikely to understand or to follow the real messages symbolized in the flower. In other words, those steeped in fundamentalist doctrinal matters so fully as to think and live separately and clannishly are blinded to the messages. The rose's messages are not for zealots of any religion; nor are the messages for the avaricious. Simply put, the rose signifies too much for those steeped in zealotry, provincialism and greed to sense or to manifest. The frequency of the rose, as rendered by nature, is higher than any particular religion or dogma, its messages apparently transcend particular belief systems and cultures as contributors to this collection have made cogently clear. Is there a final word on the rose? Seemingly so as we will see later. Clearly, there is much more to reflect upon and to understand as will be made clearer to each individual who comes, in time, intimately to know the flower. The evidence is that each person who strives for higher awareness has the potential to know all that the rose symbolizes as it points the way to intensification of consciousness and I dare say, ultimately to eternal life. This is no small feat. As we have seen in this collection of essays so far, a number of extraordinary human beings came to know the arcane life of the rose and those myriad aspects of what the flower signifies. As a companion to the previous essay about world class individuals who have embraced the impeccable flower in their work, this chapter has as its focus the rose's presence in important sacred literature. Again, we meet high level human beings connected in someway to the rose and in doing so pose the question: why is it that these people are all unusually talented leaders, larger than life so to say? Is that by design? It is it mere happenstance? Is there some organization or association that these individuals have in common? Apparently a few human beings in the universe have been pulled toward the flower and all that it signifies, in some cases after years of odd, seemingly serendipitous experiences and occurrences that have ushered them in its direction when the time was right. Sometimes initiation to an esoteric society or fraternal group provides their introduction to the rose; sometimes not. One thing is fairly certain; the flower appears after hard work, understanding and real intent toward truth seeking begins.

Knowledge and understanding of the inconspicuous presence of the flower in sacred and esoteric literature coupled with vignettes of little-known human beings who've encountered it, lead the way to insights of the rose's cosmic, mystical realms. But the real understanding of the flower comes from serious, well intended, continued work on one-self and this singular fact has been told to human beings in numerous places, veiled and unveiled. Thorns on the stem of the rose mean that some of what the flower signifies—its hidden sacred knowledge is most assuredly not intended for the profane—that is people who cannot see themselves, who do not regard others and who have not reached some measure of discipline in every aspect of their lives.

The rose is spread out in a quiet presence all over the universe, in important sometimes veiled literary passages and scriptures for those "who have eyes to see." The flower has had an overt presence in *OAHSPE,* a unique and little known nineteenth century Bible, has been alluded to in *The Secret Doctrine,* Helena Blavatsky's two-volume opus that ushered in the late nineteenth century theosophical movement, and is alluded to in *The Emerald Tablets* said to be an otherworldly document that pre-dates Christianity; and it even appears twice in some versions of the *Christian Holy Bible.* Yes, the evidence is that this quietly perfect flower has a varied presence all over the universe, in what appear to be spiritually inspired documents serving diverse cultures as far back as the lost colony of Atlantis dating thousands of years before the time mark created with the birth of Christ. The flower's veiled presence in some versions of the *Christian Holy Bible is* remarkable too, mostly because the verses containing mention of the rose in metaphor in the books *Song of Songs* and in *Isaiah* are generally misinterpreted and apparently misunderstood. [61] From diverse cultures the world over, people know at least something about the red rose: that it is lovely in the universe to touch, to smell, to enjoy and even to eat. But the masses are oblivious to veiled revelations of this ever present flower and to oblique, quiet references to it in important, urgent literature from various cultures and religions. Inimitable and timeless, the rose apparently has a cosmic connection as no other earthly flower, except perhaps its counterpart, the lotus of the East, that is said to have a thousand petals and has even been referred to as the rose-lotus. The two flowers appear to be synonymous when it comes to matters of metaphysics and higher consciousness, although some groups such as the Order of the Golden Dawn use both the lotus and the rose in different ways during ceremonies.[62] To stay on point, what are the messages to be conveyed by the rose and for whom are the revelations intended? Well, undoubtedly, to underscore the point, the rose has been "planted" to tell humans something providential and essential from the universe—from Cosmic Conscientiousness. In order to get the messages clearly, commercial qualities of the rose have to be put aside and this essential floral essence has to be seen as an exemplar of perfection and readiness to serve human beings in natural beauty and quiet perfection. These are precisely the qualities that human beings were intended to provide for each other and to the universe. Most human beings have clearly failed to create on earth or even to work fully toward all the good that the rose symbolizes in the universe from the smallest, most simple wild rose that is appreciated and used by Native Americans to the giant rose nebula, thousands of miles away in the cosmos.

The rose must be viewed as a profoundly symbolic link to divine aspects of the universe, as a sort of quantum theology in a flower. A select few in every generation have understood the messages and have attempted to live and even to teach the messages to those who are ready or astute enough to understand. Some human beings have been pulled toward the rose close enough to brush against it so to speak, but most never know its full splendor. Social philosopher Jacob Needleman addresses something of this phenomenon of never quite getting there, never quite making the connection to higher consciousness in his new book *Why Can't We Be Good?* "The obligation that is offered to us is to strive with all our being to serve what is good—while at the same time, also with all our being, to suffer in full consciousness the naked fact that it is beyond our strength. Then and only then can moral power be given to us."[63] As some reading this collection of essays may see, the symbolic messages of the rose are profoundly serious and are concerned as much with matters of culture, world peace and inner harmony as with individual aspiration to connect with the Divine as these goals are truly all interconnected and infused as highly evolved people come to cogently understand. One is able to glean this through connecting dots, to use a popular metaphor, and through the "understanding" and higher intuition that transcend the material world. Insights begin to come slowly after sincere work in the "right" direction. The essential, profound, "right" fact is that living in the material world with inner harmony and service to others while simultaneously aspiring to make the divine connection are simply flip sides of the same coin. Put another way,

human beings are supposed to learn to work on inner harmony and at the same time to work together to connect with
each other to make the earth a better place to live for all. This
is truly multi-strata work that is to be undertaken daily without too much fanfare simply because it is the "right" thing to
do, not because reward is expected. Of course these very messages are replete in all of the sacred literature, but have been
glossed over in preference for the empty dogma of religions
and material hankerings of human beings that actually mean
little in the realms of seriously higher awareness. The Work
referred to here is really important and requires discipline
to accomplish. Even those who understand what ought to be
done have a difficult time doing the work consistently—that
is simultaneously disciplining and harmonizing themselves
and working to make the world a better place. A classic little
book in metaphysics from the eastern perspective, *The Secret
of the Golden Flower* comments cogently on these profound,
essential missions that must be understood and done in tandem. One done without the other doesn't amount to much:
"Mastery of the inner world, with relative contempt for the
outer, must inevitably lead to great catastrophes. Mastery of
the outer world, to the exclusion of the in inner, delivers us

over to the demonic forces of the latter and keeps us barbaric despite all outward forms of culture."[64] Those paying attention can find plenty of examples of the barbaric in the world today as in centuries past. So much of what human beings do to each other and to themselves is a horror show that repeats or recycles generation after generation even among so-called highly civilized and educated people. Simply recall the lack of civility in our daily lives; some of what is happening now is surreal. Warmongering, hate crimes and domestic abuse are apparently on the rise worldwide. And because inner quiet and harmony are also indispensable to higher consciousness, the noise and negative vibrations emitted from over usage of cell phones, computers, ipods and, of course, high tech weapons actually hamper human beings from connection to the Source. Before he died, controversial writer, social activist Norman Mailer made a frontal assault on organized religion and forged a new catechism that links contemporary technology to weaponry of the devil.[65] Russian native, Daniel Andreev writing secretively while in a gulag in the 1940s also concluded that so much of what new technology offers is an abomination that will be used ultimately to oppress and hurt unsuspecting citizens worldwide.

Big governments and religions have failed to take responsibility to bring human beings truly together. In fact, it is becoming more obvious that walls have actually been engineered to separate human beings. Too often steeped in propaganda, dogma and zealotry, religious and governmentally engineered divides have been impediments to the right and good work that must be done to raise the collective consciousness. The earth has been divided in such a fashion that immense, impenetrable walls ensure that chaos and tension remain the rule rather than the exception. There seems little hope that human beings will ever know universal harmony. We have actually been socialized and taught for thousands of years to prefer fighting and loathing to caring about each other. Basking in varying degrees of discord, war, hatred, and selfishness perpetuated very well by governments, religions and a few powerful individuals is a lot more profitable than building bridges to bring people to the round table of peace and concord. Those who deal in arms and weapons are having a grand old time working in tandem with a bevy of officials and their associates to make loads of money and to control, oppress and even punish citizens for no high or divine purpose other than avarice. [66] Propaganda and dogma are skillfully used by a few high leaders to maintain a status quo that is divisive, anti-democratic, self-serving and more and more counterproductive. War mongering divides have been created that go on and on, far beyond so-called lifetimes. *"My God is better than your God and I know him better than you do and will proselytize, oppress you or even kill you to prove it"* seems to be the way of the world. How dumb of human kind not to work toward and demand peace, cooperation and love. Ironically, former United States President and high ranking World War II era military officer, Dwight Eisenhower is often remembered as having said people want peace so badly that sooner or later governments will have to move over and let them have it. To Eisenhower can be added a number of world class human beings, many of whom have witnessed war first-hand and have come to realize that something is out of kilter and has been for a very long time. We seem at times now to be in a slow self destruct, ironically led by organized religion and avaricious governments backed by a few powerful individuals who will not modify their greed agendas for the good of all.

Leo Tolstoy, a Russian aristocrat and Crimean War (1853–1856) era military officer also realized the importance of peace and cooperation and wrote about these powerful ideas very convincingly in a masterful work entitled *The Kingdom of God Is Within You*. Tolstoy explained that when "war breaks out, in six months the generals have destroyed the work of twenty years of effort, of patience and of genius." Tolstoy had seen war and knew its horrors well enough to make clear his conviction that it created wretched, horrible situations and, moreover, that it resulted from the "most hideous materialism."[67] Whether Tolstoy embraced the rose symbolically or not, he seemed to know something of its real essence as did his compatriot Daniel Andreev mentioned in the previous chapter. In America, Civil Rights leader Martin Luther King, Jr. also understood the rose's messages very well, although he is not ostensibly linked to the flower in any particular literature. Dr. King often used mountains as a metaphor in his speeches such as in his famous "I Have a Dream" speech. In using mountains as a metaphor, he was alluding to human beings, all, getting to a higher place where they can see the full picture: that we're all connected, all part of the same Source. We have witnessed in this anthology that a few people worldwide know the rose and have come to the realization that, in addition to its symbolic cultural connections, it signifies our interconnectedness and potential for higher consciousness. Still, the masses are easily led to war and they seem, as crazy as it may be, content with divisiveness and war. Too often religious fundamentalism becomes zealotry; people set themselves up to think that their religion or denomination is better than any other. With pomposity, too many human beings act as if they or their groups know God better than anyone else; down through the ages some have been inclined to bash heads to prove their God awareness. Inside too many churches and denominations people are jealous, unkind and mean spirited toward each other; outside their own groups, it gets worse: they want to harm each other. History teaches us that a lot of blood curdling violence has been committed in the name of religion. Such behavior most assuredly is not the way to know God or to reach Cosmic Consciousness that is one and the same.

A recent *New York Times Magazine* article written by Mark Lilla, professor of humanities at Columbia University in New York City reminds us that after all, theology is nothing but "a set of reasons people give themselves for the way things are and the way they ought to be."[68] Too often unscrupulous, avaricious leaders have run a show so to say that divides people rather than bringing them together.[69] Mankind suffers remarkably because of immense social and psychological separations engineered by churches, political and social organizations and avaricious governmental leaders. Those who lead do not exhibit the magnanimous, kind and tolerant behavior necessary to mend tense situations. Apparently, some of the leaders do not know any better themselves; at other times it would appear that divides are purposely, willfully created. Not good. Professor Lilla reminds us of the teachings of English philosopher Thomas Hobbes: "Messianic theology eventually breeds messianic politics"[70] thus warmongers know they can ultimately sell the masses almost anything, including rank aggression of other nations and human beings because "citizens" the world over buy the notion that redemption is always possible after the mega foolishness and killing sprees known as war. Lilla reminds us too of the wars that have resulted from religious fervor and our failure to see the real core of doctrinal literature, that we "must change our lives." We need, first and foremost, to work on ourselves to be better people at all times and in all places. This unheeded, high message is at the core of all of the major religions and metaphysical movements. Few get the message.

Unusual, mystical qualities of the rose stretch back over centuries and in diverse geographic locations as we've seen elsewhere in these essays. Italian poet Dante's acknowledgement of the flower as a sublime component of his initiation in *Divine Comedy* and Rumi's magnificent use of the rose as a metaphor for cosmic conscientiousness in his 13th century Persian poetry are other extraordinary examples in this collection of the flower's global pervasiveness.[71] Pointing further to mysterious aspects of the rose, James Gaffarel in 1650 noted that it had even an "astral-light" body that actually outlived the life of the flower. It is not clear what prompted Gaffarel to experiment with the flower's aura, but he found something startling: when the ashes of a burnt rose were preserved and held over a lighted candle, it became a dark cloud, still in the shape of a rose, "so Faire, so Fresh, and so Perfect a one, that you would have thought it to have been as Substantial and Odoriferous a rose as grows on a rose-tree."[72] While we know nothing of Gaffarel's state of mind or level of higher awareness, his experience with the rose is only somewhat unique as he recorded it nearly 500 years ago. Others, like Gaffarel, at various times and in a variety of places globally have also had remarkable rose encounters.

More recently, the purest essential oil of the rose has been recognized as perhaps the one and only natural oil essence that can raise the electromagnetic frequency of human beings to 320 MHz. Human beings rally around 58 MHz and frequencies lower than 32 imply shutting down of the human body, death. Dr. David Stewart, a scientist, teacher and former minister in the protestant tradition may be the first in modern times to educate human beings of the power of rose oil. The author of *The Chemistry of Essential Oils Made Simple*, Dr. Stewart notes that the oil of the rose contains 11% alkanes an important hydrocarbon and other properties that render it unique in comparison to others.[73] The alkanes of the rose supposedly have properties that are not fully understood by chemists, but these contain "spiritual and healing qualities have been recognized and applied for thousands of years." Thus pure rose oil when anointed with good intent is thought to be precious and indispensable.

Perhaps even more mysterious than Gaffarel's astral-light experience with the rose or Dr. Stewart's findings about the chemical components of rose petals, is a series of paranormal episodes experienced by a physician and dentist known as Dr. John Ballou Newbrough during the last years of the nineteenth century. Newbrough was born in Ohio in 1828, attended Cincinnati Medical College and advanced quickly as a result of a superior mind and training first in medicine and then in dentistry. He was also gifted in the paranormal from teenage years onward. Gaining financial independence during the California 1849 gold rush, Newbrough married the sister of a prospecting friend and settled in New York City where he practiced medicine and connected with a spiritualist group. Newbrough's clairvoyant and clairaudient powers were sharpened as he delved into contacting "out of body intelligences" but by his own admission he remained "disgusted with the low grade of intelligence displayed by them."[74] In other words, it appears that Newbrough wanted to advance faster than his spiritual guides were leading him, a fact also true of Elizabeth Haich who admits in her book *Initiation* that she begged for help of a master to be advanced cosmic consciousness.[75] Apparently some human beings are chosen for initiation to higher realms; others seek initiation but are denied. Why this is the case is not easily understood but it can be deduced through the study of metaphysics that past life Karma, akashic records, and sincere heartfelt intent all have a bearing on illumination. So too do hard work, service, silence and discipline of one's body, including diet. Nevertheless, between 1871 and 1881, while living in New York City in the vicinity of what is now Pennsylvania Station, Dr. Newbrough is said to have received "spiritual guidance" toward purification to the extent that he was told to stop eating meat, to discipline himself and to purchase a typewriter, an instrument that had just been introduced to the marketplace, which he did. As the little known Newbrough story goes:

> Upon sitting at the instrument an hour before dawn he discovered that his hands typed without his conscious control. In fact he was not aware of what his hands typed unless he read what was being printed. He was told that he was to write a book—but must not read what he was writing until it was completed. At the end of a year when the manuscript was completed he was instructed to read and publish the book titled *OAHSPE*, a new Bible.[76]

With guided hands, what Dr. Newbrough produced from that new typewriter was a strange, absolutely remarkable bible known by a select few as OAHSPE. It consisted of 36 books, over 800 pages, a number of illustrations, pictographs and was a provocative rendering to say the least. One of the books or chapters in *OAHSPE* known as *"Cosmogony and Prophecy"* tells "what light, heat, electricity, gravity, etc. [are] and what causes them, what holds planets in their places, gives the many cycles of time used by the ancients in their tables of prophecy and tells of relativity" and more. Another segment, The *Book of Jehovih's Kingdom on Earth* is cogent in its instructions to human beings who want to "develop spiritual powers, prophetic abilities and extra sensory perception." One warning is particularly clear and cogent: humans ought to stop eating blood thirsty carnivorous animals and stick to "herbivorous foods."[77] Prophetically, the *Book of Jehovi's Kingdom on Earth* warns of "a disease [that] came among the cows and the physicians forbade the babes being fed on their milk." Corn and rice milk were suggested as "an excellent liquid food for infants."[78] Otherwise, the same book admonishes humans to know the importance of learning: "And ye know that all light is progressive. Ye cannot settle down, saying I know enough."

The Book of Discipline provides general instructions as to how humans are to treat each other: *very well*. Discipline in all matters is a key aspect of quantum connection. A verse in the *Book of Discipline* is cogent in its message that connection to cosmic conscientiousness is possible by abandoning "earthly habits and desires" and "by constantly putting away the conditions below."[79]

A lot of what is written in *OAHSPE* makes good sense. Some of it is so other worldly as to be indecipherable. Remarkably a number of chapters of *OAHSPE* contain short passages using the metaphor of the rose; there are even pictographs of a rose in some books, most notably in *The Book of Saphah* that contains the Tablet of Hy'yi:

> Behold, the rose, deep rooted in the earth,
>   Jehovih riseth in majesty of All
> Light. His colors no man maketh, nor
>   knowth any man the cause. This subtle
> Perfume, whence cometh it, and whither
>   goeth it? What power fashioneth it,
> And propelleth it?[80]

The message that the rose is rooted deep in the earth has multiple meanings, two of which are inherent in this essay. The first and most important prong of the message alludes to the human potential to open unseen chakras or energy centers of the body.[81] These chakras open like a flower when a person has done continual sincere work on themselves, service to others and has overwhelming pure intent to reach Cosmic Consciousness or what is known commonly in the Protestant world as Christ Consciousness. People who have accomplished some level of work seemingly have a glow or radiance about them that is sometimes noticed by others but especially comes to the attention of those who have worked on higher awareness. Unevolved humans in the presence of these special "light" beings simply note that they are "different." What's more another distinguishing characteristic is that such individuals avoid the fray and foolishness of material life. We have also taken note in several chapters of this collection that the rose has important medicinal value and that its scent is invaluable. In *OAHSPE*, the pictorial referred to as the Tablet of Hy'yi in *The Book of Saphah* is perhaps decipherable for those who have had consistent study of metaphysics or theosophy. The interpretation given here is quite likely the first ever to be given in print. Page 618, plate 81 of *OAHSPE* contains a very large rose at the bottom of a pictograph and at the top of the same illustration is a crown with a cross at the top. In rectangular shape, the pictograph has two hearts just at the top of the rose. A circle with a single straight line drawn through is nestled between the two hearts. The same circle symbol is also seen in Helena P. Blavatsky's *The Secret Doctrine* and is explained there in Volume II on page 30 as in connection to the root-race of the "sweat-born." Above the circle symbol is an eye and a diamond that in all probability signifies the light or ultimate perfection that a human being comes to know through the practice of pure unconditional love on earth that is essential to rise up, incorporeally, to celestial heights. Rising up is indicated in the pictograph by what is above the moon and star in the pictograph: a crown that is sure to signify cosmic conscientiousness. Not tangential to the pictograph is the fact that a perfect diamond is referred to by the diamond industry as a paragon and contains 100 carats or more, obviously when this state is reached the rose is fully opened because it has found light. In other words, we can deduce that when a human being works really hard to overcome the material world and to love and to serve other humans and to develop a sense of community, that being may potentially rise up toward a connection with cosmic consciousness or what has been termed by some as Christ Consciousness. In Volume II (*Anthropogensis*) of *The Secret Doctrine*, HPB explains that humans have the potential to drop the external shape surrounding them or to cease to be of the material world—that is to become absolutely Divine. There is enough evidence that this process can and does take place on earth as in the obvious example of the Holy Spirit mysteries connected with lives of Jesus Christ, Mirtha and others. There are among us masters yet and still, but their presence can be sensed only by those in true service and deeply committed to the work that must be done. In this regard, today a number of groups such as Eckincar and even governments are interested in the process of rising up or detaching from one's own body, also controversially known as astral travel or as those in the world of military internationally call it, remote viewing.[82] While it has been proven that some evolved human beings actually have this capability, astral travel does not necessarily infer illumination or full initiation into Cosmic Consciousness, the so-called eternal life. Much has been written about the process of rising up to the realm of the masters; but extremely few are invited into this region. By all accounts, to move in this direction requires extraordinary discipline, inner harmony and good intent toward others. Discord and lack of good works are sure ways not to be connected to higher consciousness.

A number of verses in *OAHSPE* mention the rose briefly in a simple connection to the strive for perfection. *The Book of Apollo*, for instance, beseeches readers to "Behold the rose and the lily; they are perfect in their order. Being one with Jehovih, they painted not themselves." This book advises "symmetry of flesh; the symmetry of spirit; the harmony of music, [and that humans should] "consider wisely their behavior." Once again, this message is contained in practically all sacred literature although it is one of the most unheeded revelations in the universe.

A paradoxical footnote to the work of Dr. Newbrough is that he attempted to establish a utopian community known as Shalam near Las Cruces, New Mexico in 1884 in order to teach others to practice many of the precepts of perfection outlined in *OASPHE*. All encompassing for Newbrough and his friend Andrew Howland, Shalam was one of many utopian communities begun in America in the 19th century. Howland and Newbrough put their life savings into the community dedicated to training a diversity of orphaned children to be disciplined and spiritually exceptional. The successes were remarkable as described by Lee Priestly who has researched the Shalam community:

> Naturally the spiritual development of the children was of prime importance. In addition to the study of *OAHSPE*, they were taught the means of communicating with angels and how to discriminate between good and evil spirits. At the ages of twelve to fourteen they were initiated into the rites and ceremonies of the Ancients with explanation of appropriate signs, symbols and emblems. Trances and manifestations were common-place to them. They received spirit messages and responded to rappings and table tippings.[83]

According to Priestly's research, the children were also taught manners and decorum. The children were the focal point of the community and were trained to be unfailingly polite, but not forward. They conversed with adults easily and with poise; among themselves they were loving and non-competitive.[84] Unfortunately, the same can not be said of the adults of the community known as Faithists. Not surprisingly, the adult group at Shalam was described by Priestly as men and women who at that time shirked labor, expected something for nothing, lounged idly and were known generally to be quarrelsome and critical. As described by Priestly, the 19th century initial group has no reflection on contemporary Faithists groups which still exist in the United States.

At age 63 in April 1891 Newbrough and a number of the children at Shalam died of la grippe, a particularly virulent disease so named because of the horrible grip it had on some American communities at the end of the century. With Howland at the helm, the Shalam community lumbered along for over a decade after Newbrough's death but was beset with law suits and bickering among the adults who lived there. Howland was said to be fair and reasonable and he introduced many new vegetables and fruits to the area, but was not a manager of the caliber Newbrough had been. Noted for his strange attire of white pantaloons and preferring a long flowing white beard, Howland was arrested twice for "indecent exposure." [85] Shalam folded in 1907.

Perhaps stranger than fiction or mere coincidence, Helena Petrovna Blavatsky, also telepathic and one of the founders of the worldwide Theosophical movement, died the same year as Dr. Newbrough in 1891. As noted earlier, Newbrough was born in Ohio in 1828 while his contemporary, Blavatsky, was born in Russia in 1831. There is no evidence that the two knew each other. They traveled in different circles, he in the United States and Australia and she in India, the United States and all over Central Europe where *The Secret Doctrine* was penned. The evidence is that *The Secret Doctrine,* well over 2600 pages, was actually spiritually dictated to Blavatsky while she resided in several locations including in Elberfeld, Germany, Ostend, Belgium and around England with Countess Constance Wachtmeister as her companion a good portion of the time. The two were frequently in the company of visitors from the Theosophical Society who were witnesses to some of the unusual circumstances surrounding Blavatsky's work on the opus.[86] By HPB's own account she was visited by an ascended master in 1851 while visiting Hyde Park in London with her father for the first time; she was quite young at the time, only 17 years old.[87] It is generally thought that HPB's guide was Master Morya who is said to be the head of "all of the esoteric schools which truly prepare an aspirant for ashramic contact and work." [88] But long before 1851 there was a lot of drama and mystery surrounding the privileged Russian woman known as HPB among theosophists. To add to her mystique, she is known to have run away from a seventy-five year old retired military husband at age 17 after declaring herself a widow who "wouldn't be a slave to God Himself, let alone man." [89] Known to have a hot temper, Blavatsky was undoubtedly an oddity by all accounts. Those who came into her orbit were likely to witness some very strange, unexplainable things wherever she was around; by all accounts she was much stranger than her contemporary Dr. Newbrough. Because she was so remarkably unusual, stories about her are kept alive because a number of people were aware of her "gifts" and tracked her from an early age. Key among those tracking HPB were members of her family. Known as Helene von Hahn at birth, HPB was recognized as a medium from her childhood years and known for very high intellect in the years after her mother's death in 1842. She was also "the strangest girl one has ever seen, one with a distinct dual nature…one mischievous, combative, and obstinate—everyway graceless; the other as mystical, metaphysically inclined. ...No schoolboy was ever more uncontrollable or full of the most unimaginable pranks...".[90] Manly Hall's insightful article about her in The Phoenix benefited from the journal notes of HPB's aunt in Russia:

> It was as though a troop of sprites were in constant attendance, ever mindful of her bidding. Her uncanny prophetic powers by turns amazed and discomfited visitors for looking them intently in the face, like some Pythoness or Delphi, in half-formed childish words she would solemnly predict the place and time of their death... [H]er prognostications were socorrect that she became the terror of the domestic circle. Nothing could concealed from her that she desired to know. She could read the most hidden thoughts and motives and was constantly aware of circumstances occurring at a distance.[91]

Dr. Newbrough, it may be recalled, was also approached psychically in a preliminary visit from a master, but much later in his life than HPB and closer to the time he was actually dictated his one and only opus, *OAHSPE*. There is no evidence that either HPB or Newbrough was fearful or apprehensive about undertaking the tasks given them by masters. While there are some similar aspects in the way the two were approached, there is no evidence that Blavatsky was asked to be careful of her diet or to purchase a typewriter as Newbrough had been instructed. Other than both being "visited" preliminarily years in advance of the major tombs they were guided to write, the only other noteworthy similarity is that both Newbrough and HPB were plagued by scandal and charged by "outsiders" as being impostors. It could be reasoned that Blavatsky's reputation suffered most from scandal since her work came to the attention of theosophists, non-theosophists and even the global press followed her work rather closely. The attempts to discredit HBP are not surprising since she was guided from an other worldly source that few human beings can comprehend then or now. As Manly Hall explained in an early issue of *The Phoenix*, "humanity attacks viciously and relentlessly anyone who assails the infallibility of the mediocre." What's more, "The fear is not that the occultist may be wrong; the fear is that the occultist may be right."

Ironically, the information dictated to Blavatsky contained two major divisions known as *Cosmogenesis* (Volume I) and *Anthropogenesis* (Volume II) which are also aspects of the voluminous revelations dictated to Newbrough. Writing, terminology and organization of the two books are vastly different and *OAHSPE* contains far more illustrations than *The Secret Doctrine*_but both are clearly major works that have been overlooked by the masses. It is pure conjecture to say that both works have been reserved for or intended for a select few, but it would appear that is the case. Is it mere coincidence that the symbol of the rose appears quietly in both *OAHSPE* and in *The Secret Doctrine* or that the two authors died the same year after having been given major Arcanum or keys to understanding the cosmological foundations of the universe? What Newbrough and Blavatsky provided apparently far exceeds the cosmological and anthropological insights presented in any other religious or sacred literature, yet few are aware of their respective works, *OAHSPE* and *The Secret Doctrine*. Ironically, HPB and Newbough were only three years apart in age; she died at age 60 and he at 63.

Of course there is now and always has been a great deal of conjecture and speculation about the so-called lost continent of Atlantis; but highly astute, great minds such as Plato and Helena Petrovna Blavatasky say firmly that the continent did indeed exist. Whatever one thinks of HPB's pronouncements about Atlantis or the oddities surrounding her life, she was undeniably a great intuitive and was recognized widely as such. Blavatsky explained that "axial disturbances" are part and parcel of the "intelligent Kosmic hand and law" which alone could reasonably explain such sudden changes..." [as the disappearance of Atlantis]. According to HPB's *Secret Doctrine*: "old continents were sucked in by the oceans, other lands appeared and huge mountain chains arose where there had been none before." What is the evidence of all of this? Well, Plato's *Timaeus* also discusses Atlantis in some detail that has been pretty well corroborated for those who have taken note. [92] And HPB offers, as one evidence, the very large statutes found in the Easter Islands and in the Gobi Desert that Atlantis did exist. Human-like beings over "nine yatis" or "27 feet tall" inhabited Atlantis which was the Atlantic Ocean portion of Lemuria; this was the cradle of the third root race that occupied a vast area of the Pacific and Indian oceans, according to HPB.[93] These are apparently the same large statutes depicted to the world in the Erich von Daniken controversial film *"Chariots of the Gods"* many years ago.[94] If we can concede for the purposes of this essay that Atlantis did exist, it would make sense that the giant beings who lived there were pretty smart to leave statutes reminiscent of themselves made of a rock substance that has lasted thousands and thousands of years. And it wouldn't be surprising that at least a portion of this Atlantean group was so highly evolved that they lived by a set of laws set down in a special, little-known book called *The Emerald Tablets*. The leader of this evolved group of Atlanteans in a place known as Keor was Thoth, an eternal being who knew the secrets of everlasting life and led a group of thirteen adepts who were said to be well versed in scientific and philosophical matters.[95]

In recent times, there has been renewed interest in *The Emerald Tablets* and conjecture whirls around about the origin of this obviously important work, including who fetched it back to the Pyramids in Egypt. Michael Doreal is said to be the man who revived and translated the *Tablets*. Doreal was a great if not well known spiritual leader, healer and teacher who was born Claude Dodgin in Oklahoma (USA).[96] Rather amazingly, he was thought by some to be a reincarnation of the great teacher Horlet who lived in Egypt during the time of Atlantis, at least 20,000 years ago. Although there is no evidence that the occurrences of his life were as controversial or as stupefying as those connected to Newbrough or HPB, there were some spiritual oddities, most notably the fact that he was "given" the task of retrieving the mysterious *Tablets* from the jungles of the Yucatan in a Temple of the Sun God and returning them to the Great Pyramid in Egypt. Through great peril, Doreal is said to have translated and returned the sacred, secret *Tablets* to the designated place; under his direction the book was published in English in 1939. Doreal also taught higher awareness, metaphysics courses for a number of years to a select group of males and females in Oklahoma.[97] On earth, Doreal is best known by a few as the leader of the American wing of a group known as the Temple of the White Brotherhood that has its foundation high in the Himalayas of Asia. Remarkably, *The Emerald Tablets* contains numerous mentions of a rose-like flower that has petals. By all indications, the reference is to a rose but it doesn't really matter if the flower referred to in the *Tablets* is a perfect red rose or not; the messages are cogent, clear and very much like messages in other sacred literature regarding an impeccable, revered flower. Planted in the human body are invisible flowers along a high level invisible "yellow brick road" to cosmic consciousness. The trick is to uncover the map to the path and to symbolically make roses bloom along the way through service, love and inner harmony. Notwithstanding the trials and tribulations of life, ultimately the opportunity exists to walk into the tremendous light at the end of the journey. This and only this is the essential veiled message of numerous classic stories, including *The Wizard of Oz*. It is also the ultimate message of the classic opera *The Magic Flute* and revered literature engineered to reach a diversity of the masses. Only a select few are drawn to this literature and yet, the messages have been prevalent in a variety of writing and pictographs through the centuries and longer. *The Emerald Tablets*, eons old and not surely not easily understood, have much to say about this process of making flowers bloom: "In freeing the consciousness from the body it is best to expand the solar-plexus (one of the chakras), the Flower of Life of the body, and send the life force flooding through it so that the body is vitalized in preparation for the consciousness to leave..."[98] Of course, it should be noted again that this work of making roses bloom in the human body requires intensive, well intentioned work that must be accomplished in silence. *The Emerald Tablets* underscores an important fact about higher consciousness: "He who talks does not know; he who knows does not talk." For the highest knowledge is "unutterable."

It is not surprising that the rose also makes its appearance quietly in the King James version of the Christian *Holy Bible* and also in Gnostic portions of the Bible such as *The Book of Enoch* that have been omitted, for whatever reason, from the King James version. Thought to predate the New Testament, *The Book of Enoch*, provides powerful rose metaphors such as the birth of Methuselah's strange son whose "body was white as snow and red as the blooming of a rose...[99]" Undoubtedly this metaphor references Methuselah's illumination or connection to the Holy Spirit. By now it is apparent as a result of recent discoveries and insight that the *Bible* has been altered numerous times[100] and a significant part, the Gnostic portion, has been hidden from the masses. Still the allegories, parables and metaphors contained in this revered book, if truly understood, are instructive and, to say the least, full of revelations. Quite apparently there is no other book like it on earth although it clearly is not based on historical truth or intended for literal consumption. In other words, reading the Bible and quoting from it does not automatically translate into understanding the messages contained therein. One of the beauties and enigmas of *The Holy Bible* is that it is full of dual meanings. Moreover *The Holy Bible* contains hidden knowledge, in parable, allegory and metaphor that simply is not intended for those who are not ready for it. And a lot of it has been cut out or omitted for good reason. Geoffrey Hodson, well known as a teacher and leader in theosophy explained carefully in *The Hidden Wisdom in The Holy Bible, Volume I* that there is much support for a symbolic reading of the *Bible* in, for instance, "the promises of perpetual prosperity and divine protection made by God to Abraham and his successors with subsequent defeats by invaders, exile under their commands in Babylon and Egypt and destruction of the Temples of King Solomon" etc. More recently, Episcopal Bishop John Selby Spong, author of *Rescuing the Bible from Fundamentalism, Born of a Woman* and other significant works has made clear his view that much of the Bible is misunderstood and misinterpreted by theologians. That said, it should be noted there are only two somewhat obscure, but absolutely beautiful references to the rose in *The Old Testament*: in *Song of Songs,* chapter 2 and in *Isaiah*, chapter 35, verses that are as easy to miss as they are misinterpreted and widely disputed.

Isaiah is said to be the most prophetic book of the Old Testament, revealing unique prophecies regarding Immanuel and the "Suffering Servant." The prophet Isaiah is also said to have been a literary genius. Of all the prophets he is said to have looked further into the future than any other as is revealed in this book of *The Old Testament*. According to some sources, he lived a long time, even through the reign of three kings and was even an advisor to one of them, Hezekiah, from 729 to 699 B. C.

The 35th Chapter of Isaiah, verse one uses the rose in metaphor. It reads "the desert shall rejoice, and blossom as the rose." In translation, the metaphor means after the necessary work has been completed, the tribulation period will be over and blessings will flow. This verse has nothing to do with a desert per se and this is obvious to the astute reader. One interpretation puts it another way: "all spiritual evil and physical catastrophe will be reversed and the land and people will be blessed." In fact, the book of Isaiah is replete with this same message in veil: we all have the potential to connect with the Holy Spirit, if we reverse our courses, slay the ego, care for one another, and work fully toward the light. When this is accomplished even the "tongue of the dumb will sing" to use another metaphor for rising up out of the material realm which brings everlasting joy and no "sorrow and sighing."

A bevy of biblical scholars have offered interpretations of the *Song of Songs*, including: allegorical, typological, anthology of love songs, three-character interpretation and literal love story, but the overall purpose is said "to show the joy of married love as a gift of a good and loving God."[101] All of the interpretations seem plausible, but from this writer's perspective none of them get at the real meaning, the hidden message of this most beautifully written book of the Old Testament. Like countless other dual meaning verses in the Bible, verses about the rose have multiple meanings. Apparently this was the intended result because, like the sages and mystics before him, Jesus taught in parables and the Bible is fully allegorical and metaphoric. Clearly, contained therein are sacred, arcane messages intended for a select few; one has only to look at the murder, mayhem, avarice and lack of humility in the world today to understand why mystics were careful not to waste time on "gross wits" and on those who refused to do the necessary work.[102]

At a glance *Song of Songs* has been interpreted to be erotic verse or even a love song sung about two lovers; the shepherd-king and his beloved outcast maiden. The story goes that after a period of absence, the former shepherd Solomon returns as King and takes the maiden away with him in a royal coach to become his bride. This quiet verse is reminiscent of Rumi's poetry. The essential point to be made is found in the manner in which Solomon and his maiden embrace each other; in verse 13 of chapter one, for instance, she wants him "betwixt her breasts." But there is nothing carnal in her wishes. The metaphor between her breasts means transcending this world. Getting beyond duality that so drives the nature of human beings, or for those who've studied the Law of the Three in Sacred Geometry, it is getting beyond the polarity of the material world. In the tradition of Taoist teachings, getting between the maiden's breasts would be tantamount to getting beyond the yin and the yang or the dual nature of man to transcend the material world. As human beings move toward objective conscience, higher and higher levels can be achieved, usually over lifetimes up to merger with the Divine, far beyond the duality that so plagues humans on a daily basis. In the book *Song of Songs*, if the King can get between, indeed beyond the maiden's breasts, he will get better than all the "other daughters" can possibly render unto him meaning metaphorically of course that the King will simply have overcome the material world. Here there is nothing erotic intended though at a glance it would seem so. In Chapter 2, verses one, two and three using the rose as a most powerful metaphor the maiden steadfastly declares that she is the best:

> I am the rose of Sharon and the lily of the
> valleys, so is my love among the daughters
> as the apple tree among the trees of the
> wood, so is my beloved among sons. I sat
> down under his shadow with great delight,
> and his fruit was sweet to my taste.

If this most beautiful verse of *The Old Testament* was put in the vernacular of today, the translation would be that the maiden referred to in *Song of Songs* is "a knock out," she's so well built, so fantastic, has it "going on" to the point that none of the other "daughters" or females in the community measure up to her. Such is the case metaphorically when one reaches Cosmic Consciousness, nothing else measures up;

after the connection is made everything is magical and perfect. Nothing else is desired or needed! One literally and figuratively rises up above this material world, above this earth to connect with the source. What Dante, Rumi, Hanai, the prophet Isaiah and King Solomon all seem to know, few of us are capable grasping and certainly are not capable of doing the disciplined work to realize: there is absolute perfection if and when one ratchets up to the Holy Spirit. There is no denying that the Spirit is the key and it takes work to connect with it.[103] Sadly millions upon millions attend mosques, churches, masses and perform other religious rituals daily and have not come to understand this profound fact. The kind of attendance needed is attendance to oneself to be a better human being and to connect with respect and kindness to each other, not necessarily attendance at any particular service, religion or sect.

Considering the extraordinary occurrences and facts unfolded in the essays of this collection, all is still not said and done about the rose; there are yet other odd components of this most quintessential flower. Perhaps no aspect of the flower's symbolism is more striking and perhaps confusing than its connection to Parseeism or Perseism, the worship of defied fire. This is not fire in a literal sense, according to Hargrave Jennings, it is "the inexpressible something of which real fire or rather its flower" is symbolized in the rose. Fire worship is an odd belief system and philosophy that rarely even makes its way to philosophy textbooks today and yet it has been a component of pagan and primitive worship for thousands of years and continues in some traditions even today. As strange as it may seem, this connection to fire is one of the early justifications for the practice of cremation which has been around for thousands of years.[104] Even the torches used at early funerals were not solely for light. Torches, light, candles and so on when used in sacred services are of course the "inexpressible mystery of the Holy Ghost."

Fire has had a strange history in religion and metaphysics. The realities of fire's connection to the realms of religion, metaphysics and God seeking in general have actually been stranger than fiction could be, ever. The world over, for thousands of years, people haven't known quite how to make their connections to God or cosmic consciousnesses so that they make up stuff as they go along, some of it so macabre as to be mind numbing. Some humans, over epochs, have quite apparently had a huge crazy misunderstanding about the meaning of fire in connection to religion and God-seeking. Centuries ago, and perhaps even now in some places in the universe, people actually burned animals, themselves and even each other as sacrificial offerings in attempts to curry favor with God or at least their gods.[105] At times self-immolation or sacrifice has been practiced in Indian and Tibetan Buddhism and in some sects of the Middle East, the whole purpose of which was thought to be a way of leaving the material body. All of the sacrificial rituals and goings on have been most assuredly unnecessary and a perversion of what was intended. While fire symbolically relates to Spirit, undeniably, it is not to be taken literally; self immolation profits one nothing. The point of the best theology, too often veiled, is to learn to live together in harmony and also to find inner peace. When these two goals can be accomplished in tandem by individuals, a light comes on and gets brighter and brighter—that is to say an internal, invisible flower opens and the individual potentially becomes one with Spirit.

The Holy Bible (St. James version), has numerous metaphors and allegories related to fire, most notably in the book of Daniel: "a fiery stream issued and came forth before him..." from this biblical verse we note that the manifestation of God was fire or Spirit. And the book of Matthew warns that man baptizes with water, but eventually "He shall baptize you with the power and glory and with fire." What kind of God would appear as fire and also promise to baptize humans as fire and not with water? For the fire philosophers, the answer to that question was easy: a God who is one with the Holy Spirit and is the Source of All and Everything. As Michael Doreal explained in his interpretation of *The Emerald Tablets*, "Man's destiny is the final blending with light even though he moves through darkness during material incarnations." [106] This is the essence of why some cultures have preferred cremation and why fire has been a component of burial ceremonies. It is also sadly, for the misguided, the reason for self immolation. Thus the "signification of fire burial is the commitment of human mortality into the last of all matter, overleaping the intermediate states; or delivering over of the man-unit into the Flame-Soul, past all intervening spheres or stages of the purgatorial.[107] Surely fire symbolizes the Holy Spirit and, as we have seen throughout this anthology, the rose symbolizes much but nothing so urgent and important as its connection to fire that is symbolic of the Divine. When the magnificent rose opens to the light, or put another way when petals of all of the invisible chakras in the human body open to the light of what is good and harmonious this symbolizes that connection with the Holy Spirit or Cosmic Consciousness has been achieved.

The great philosopher, alchemist, physician Philip Theosophratus Aureolous Bombast Hohenheim, widely and controversially known by the name Paracelsus (1493–1541) understood the connection of fire to the Holy Spirit as is revealed in his writings and teachings. To say the least, Paraselsus did not live a charmed life. But he did live such an exciting and unusual life that stories have been written about him, including one by Argentine writer Jorge Luis Borge (1889–1986) titled "*The Rose of Paracelsus.*" In the Borge's story a doctor (Paracelsus) has asked God for a disciple and one appears who is apparently full of doubts because he asked for evidence so that he would know for certain if he ought to follow the great doctor. In the story Paracelsus listens intently to the disciple's request for evidence—that is a request that he turn a rose into ashes and make it reappear which the great doctor declines to do. Alas, the would-be disciple leaves unconvinced that he should follow Paracelsus because he did not see the rose converted to ashes. After the disciple exits, Paracelsus quietly makes the rose appear from the ashes.

The moral of the story seems to be that if humans doubt the power of the rose, the power of the Holy Spirit, then it's not for them and the connection cannot be made. Known as an efficient astrologist, alchemist and philosopher, Paraselsus was also a preacher who addressed crowds in taverns in a mix of religion and political polemic that called for social equality based on Christian principles.[108] In words that are as apropos today as they were during the Renaissance years in which he lived, Paracelsus warned "No good can happen to the poor with the rich being what they are. They are bound together as with a chain. Learn you rich, to respect these chains. If you break your link, you will be cast aside."[109] We can not deduce from the teachings of Paracelsus that he necessarily favored the poor over the rich, what he advocated was cooperation between the stratas of society and between the races, a melding of aims for the benefit of all. Ultimately, finally, such cooperation follows the spirit of the rose. It is wise for us to mimic this spirit and to be ever mindful of the Source.

Chapter Four

Gurdjieff's Third World Rose and "Okidanokh"

For the life of the flesh is in the blood; and
 I have given
It to you upon the altar to make atonement
 for your souls;
For it is the blood that maketh an atone-
 ment for the soul.

Leviticus, Chapter 17, Verse 11

Neither by the blood of goats and calves, but
 by his own blood
He entered in once into the holy place, having obtained eternal
Redemption for us.

Hebrews 9, Verse 11

That Island on which Mister God himself

and the deserving souls

Exist is called "paradise" and existence there

is just "roses,

Roses."

G. I. Gurdjieff, *Beelzebulb's Tales*, p. 217

T he concept of third world citizenship is at once politically provocative and also surprisingly mystical although this latter, higher realm is illusive or unknown to most of us. And so it is that mystical or numinous aspects of "third world" have been veiled and worse, when revealed, few humans can grasp the full gist. Explanations have been scant except in venues such as secret orders, private group work or perhaps as a result of a long monastic or meditative work. The guideposts for higher consciousness have been ever contained in ancient wisdom books and in timeless poetry.[1] Still, average humans simply

---

[1] See, for instance, the varied poetry and writings of Rumi, Attar or Dante and the ancient scriptures known as the **Upanishads**, the **Bhagavad Gita** or the oldest sacred scriptures of Hinduism, the **Rigveda**. *Recently, the sacred texts given most attention are the* **Dead Sea Scrolls***, said by one scholar-curator to be "the most significant cultural treasure of a Jewish nature."* **The Tibetan Book of the Dead**, translated by Robert A. F. Thurman is essential for its explana-

do not understand the need for regular meditation and practical, work that is necessary to achieve a *shift* in consciousness. This is the essential, necessary effort required to achieve a supreme gift from the Source. The "third world" metaphor signifies that really good Work toward balance is the essential component to rise up, far beyond the emotion-driven senses. Transformation is just the beginning of the process. And the road map has always been available for the astute, for those whose intent it is to wake up to what the epigraphs above provide only hints. Undeniably, for the vast majority of us, the map to higher consciousness has been illusive, but always present somewhere for gracefully disciplined, sincere seekers. We gain very little without balance and the sad fact is our religions, all over the globe, have not made this fact cogent.

After many years of being "churched" in several Christian denominations, it is impossible for me to recall a sermon which truly explained any of the mysteries of the blood or of the detailed, true process to higher consciousness. During

---

tion that delusion-driven life is suffering. Also insightful is Rudolf Steiner's book, *The Fifth Gospel*. Steiner explained that the mystery at Golgotha was a turning point for humans; after that heredity was not the essential condition for advancement of the soul, now we must each fend for ourselves to achieve a shift in consciousness.

decades of observing and participating in the "church" process, I noticed, even as a child, a lot of praying, various programs, rituals such as baptisms and christenings and a lot of quoting from the scriptures. But in contrast, keen note was taken of the fact that there was significant hypocrisy and other negative behaviors inside church communities. It was at mid-life, through an encounter with a Tibetan Lama, that I was to hear profoundly the same message earlier uttered by my uneducated, rather sincere and hardworking grandmother whose name was Laura. She said simply and multiple times: "God knows everything." The Lama put it more succinctly: in a person's life everything counts and matters: every thought, word and deed and even hidden intent. That simple message shook my comfort zone as has the Gurdjieff teachings which also remind me perpetually that there is a system of accountability and a hierarchy toward higher consciousness. There are real consequences for being out of emotional control and especially for doing intentional harm to others. Added to that, when it comes to the Ray of Creation, humans generally are not high up at all. I thought we were. We seemed to be. Thus, the fact that we really aren't that important in the whole of other galaxies and cosmic renderings saddens me; I have been duped like practically everybody else. Actually, this revelation was another shocker for me. I had grown up watching television actors, community leaders, and entertainers with a child's gaze and most of them seemed nothing less than extraordinarily special to my very limited world. My impression was that most of my teachers and television and movie actors were smart people, but even as a child, it was clear to me that some were smarter and had a lot more grace than others. Few of us knew then of their troubled private lives.

It is the mystical perspective of "third world" that requires humans to wake up to the stark reality that practical effort to overcome emotional responses internally and externally is involved in the process of advancement to higher spiritual realms. Real work leads to a shift in consciousness, a necessary foundation for so called eternal life. There is a distinct process to rising up, to waking up to higher consciousness. Ministers, preachers and priests cannot do this work for us and they do not remind us enough of the consequences to be faced when we drift, dillydally and dawdle our way toward death. Simply attending church, synagogues and temples is not enough. The intent and work toward growth has to be regular and surefooted. Real practical work must be accomplished with such sincerity and purity that we eventually come to the special attention of the Source, the maker of all and everything, seen and unseen. Over lifetimes, with graceful effort and good intent, there is available to us a slow rise toward initiation and ascension. Until then we are on the wheel of human existence. Not many humans seem to know about this. A few sages have written about really wicked humans being kicked off the wheel to lower worlds which bears no discussion here. I have no problem believing that a winnowing process is ever present for humans, as it is in nature. The evidence is there have been several sweeps of humans off the earth, since we mostly lag when it comes to important spiritual work. When the phenomenal feat of elevated connection or admission to the path of eternal life takes place, there will be a variety of signals such as an intense flow of sustaining, reoccurring current of vibration and the occasional appearance of a ray of light or what has been called Satva and by other names. The Source, is aided by a host of beings that some of us call Masters. All of them seem to have taught in a mostly veiled way. But, some of the signals that one is on the path of ascension can been seen and felt by a few and have been well documented.[110] Frankly, before signals are provided, a continued, heightened state of self mastery must be accomplished. The quest to "do" better or die to the old self is a solo process. We are each to learn to talk less, eat less, meditate regularly, discipline our thoughts and words and be ever so careful and discerning about all deeds. Until we strike the right balance, the real ticket out of the human quagmire, we are relegated to be born again and again, and usually suffer thru multiple lives until we learn certain lessons which must be mastered, but are different for each of us. All sincere effort counts toward moving up. Again, nobody can make effort on behalf of someone else; even prayer is tricky because humans who are out of balance and wobbly themselves do not make good, calibrated prayers. Effectively, as energetic beings we emit and attract vibratory qualities to us based on our level of being. This is an urgent and important fact to remember. Moreover, close associations with awful people can propel us toward unsavory energy unless we are well protected from it.

George I. Gurdjieff (1877–1949) realized that what was conveniently labeled "third world citizenship" in his last book, *Life is Real...*[111] is exceedingly difficult to obtain. He used the third world metaphor mostly in his commonly known "third series" but the concept is actually inherent in his other writings as well. Used as a powerful arcane metaphor, Gurdjieff used the term long before the historically significant Bandung Conference in 1955. There are surprising parallels as to what Gurdjieff intended and to what the political conference had as its intent. The Conference was planned with the mission to bring the geo-political third world together for common good. This third world political Conference, using ironically the same terminology—third world—that Gurdjieff had used several decades prior, was held in West Java, Indonesia, southeast of Djakarta. The avowed quest for mutual respect for sovereignty, strive for equality, political self-determination, and noninterference in the internal affairs of the participating countries were key aspects of the meeting. Whether the Conference was a success or not is of no issue here, but the metaphor used to convene the meeting is instructive. It called upon certain poor countries and regions to uplift, to overcome "rule" and then work on themselves after years of rule intrusions by outsiders. This term "colonial" rule serves well as a metaphor for how humans are generally like poor countries owing to the fact that we are jerked around by internal and external programming that has been well noted in Gurdjieff's teachings. Our internal, mental turmoil and outward emotional responses to other people often "rule" us. We are like those poor countries sending delegates to Bandung that wanted to overcome so-called "colonial rule." We too must overcome "rule" of emotions. The term "colonial rule" easily suffices as a metaphor to represent layers of programming which govern most humans. Gurdjieff taught that we take our "orders" from this internal and external programming, until we learn self mastery. These tiers of programming usually lead to psychological, spiritual and even physical detriment. Humans are born to suffer, one way or the other. When higher consciousness does not flow in, we are left to deal with lives were distortions abound. The obvious result of programming is that we live horizontally, with little focus on creating opportunities to rise up, to live vertically. [112] Gurdjieff's ideas about achieving third world citizenship require us to *Do* Work toward the same goals as the Bandung Conference, to overcome "rule" of internal and external programming. In this essay, we explore more of what Gurdjieff meant by "Third World" in the context of what the extraordinary results of overcoming both programs could mean for us. We are reminded that we must Work harder, better and with grace to overcome—to obtain a shift in consciousness, to tap into the silent, light-filled flow of Gurdjieff's "third world."[113] This is no small feat and there is not a lot of guidance on how to do it.

There is no reason to debate or intellectualize Gurdjieff's teachings for those who understand the real meaning and the inherent intent to overcome programming so as to achieve higher consciousness. Balance, Self Remembering, Self Observation, sitting, and sensing meditations are some of the prime concepts and methods, the foundation of what is affectionately and respectfully termed by seekers "the Work." Only a few, relatively speaking, learn that it is important to undertake practical Work toward change in order to slowly overcome programming. The nature of the Work has been addressed and well described using numerous metaphors and allegories throughout the writings of Gurdjieff and his key followers such as British psychiatrist Dr. Maurice Nicoll. In a multivolume series, Dr. Nicoll made the Work lessons more practically accessible for the times in which we live. Personally, I'm amazed to have encountered in group work a few individuals who still do not understand that we are programmed. We arrive with a script that is embellished—tweaked—as we pursue aspects of earthly life. Humans actually resist the idea of being scripted or programmed and seemingly still think they are ordinarily in charge of themselves. The idea that Karma of past incarnations is impacting them daily is totally foreign. For me, the realization that we are programmed was the prime prerequisite for beginning to overcome the programming. Until a human has this realization, the work can never really begin toward what Christians have labeled being "born again" toward the eternal life. I have become painfully aware that only a very few humans are brought to understand that we are programmed based on lack of progress—that is little work on ourselves from past lives. It would seem that most of us do not want to know about the process. If we do not have stuff to overcome (programming) why bother to be "born again"? We are driven by ego, personality, DNA, parceled out phenomenally on an individual basis through planetary forces and orchestrated by Lords of Karma, otherwise known as seven eyes. Waking up to this fact usually happens after years of study, meditation, conscious suffering and meaningful, selfless service to humanity. Most people seem to think they are acting fully on their own accord. One has only to consult with a master astrologer to figure out programming for a particular lifetime is tied to planetary forces which are dictated-orchestrated by Karma from past incarnations. The process is intricate and involved. After reviewing the planetary configuration at the time of my birth, a master astrologer advised me that I had earned a few privileges in this life that others do not have, because of previous good works. The same message was provided to me by an intuitive. This was very big news to me, but it does support that what is happening and is going to happen is already known by a few because the script is already written for each human. Thus, the process of meting out of Karma is well documented. In the Christian Gospels (Ecclesiastes 1: verse 9), for instance, it is mentioned cogently "there is nothing new under the sun," and this revelation backs up the idea of Karma. The verse says further "that which has been is what will be..." There is not enough guidance toward breaking away from this process and although much is made of consequences of acting out, doing harmful stuff, people still do not fully understand the process. To make these ideas even clearer, in Alice Bailey's important book, *Esoteric Astrology* the point is made that humans must overcome their natural predilections toward animal nature. No surprises there! Moreover, most of us are under the influence of *non*-sacred planets, which we know nothing about.[114] Sorry to say, the earth is not a sacred planet, according to Bailey's book and that would explain most of the craziness that goes on here.

Gurdjieff spread his teachings throughout parts of Europe and eventually to a few key cities in America with much verve, intrigue and some degree of inconvenience.[115] Even today, few people understand the true nature of his eso-teric teachings: observe yourself, Work for balance as a base level foundation to overcome programming, Work toward a shift in consciousness—in short, get closer to the Source, to "Endlessness" through stages and some major constrictions, seen and unseen. The process has sometimes been likened to a musical scale. Some Christians in song liken the process to climbing a ladder and still others say it leads to so called eternal life. At a glance, there are no parallels between the teachings wrought by Gurdjieff and the Conference held at Bandung in 1955, sponsored by the governments of Burma, India, Indonesia, Pakistan and Sri Lanka and twenty-four other nations from Asia, Africa and the Middle East. But the metaphors are strong and instructive. What the nations had in common was having recently overcome colonial rule. Gurdjieff taught that we too must overcome the colonial rule of both *internal* stuff of DNA (traits and Karma encoded from elsewhere) and *external* programming of sometimes hard socialization by religions, socio-economic and so-called family status, etc. Put cogently, we ought not let all of the programming morph into continued bad Karma, because this happens easily. With great effort, we are to **Do** the Work of overcoming all that conditions us to be boxed tightly to the material world of the senses and negativity to boot. We also need to overcome encoded DNA, if it is of the nature to hold us back—that's the stuff that medical science, astrologers and intuitives can tell is already written in individual human scripts. This overcoming process is big work and few in the human community seem up to the feat of accomplishing anything near it. We learn rather quickly that most of us cannot "do…" and yet some of us struggle on, at least with the desire to seek truth, to grow up vertically which is a seeking of eternity in the gospels. The lifestyle of the sense-filled world of worry and various forms of fray has to be replaced with harmony. Harmful thoughts, words, deeds simply must be overcome and replaced with light-filled good thoughts, words, deeds—a total free-will reorganization which interestingly has a reverberation effect. In other words, when we harmonize our emotions and work on ourselves, it helps others and even other nations and those far away in the cosmos, as will be explained later in this essay. In short, when we are in a good state, we emit a different vibratory quality and it impacts everything.

Most of us assume that we have a soul and, especially in the West, we hear a lot about this concept in song, poetry and in light banter about "soul mates," "soul's purpose" and such, but the real story is that a soul has to be developed. Gurdjieff reminds us that it has to be earned: "a soul is not born with man and can neither unfold nor take form in him so long as his body is not fully developed." The soul's development hinges tightly on "finer" matter which comes in from outside, sort of like DNA does. Until a process of coating takes place, we are essentially "dead" souls or put slightly milder, we are slaves to the system of DNA and to our various socializations on earth. All of this is a lot to overcome. From the perspective of Gurdjieff's teachings, **the third world is a man's own world that he has worked to *create*.** This new world that an evolved human might achieve revolves around the all-important Cosmic Law of Three. Two forces must blend in order to conceive and then to enact creation forces. Likewise, for a human on the path, there must be will, intent and work against the old way of operating in order to create something new—to overcome the lower self. This new "third world" has overcome past life stuff of DNA and attendant issues that flow in from other incarnations. Nor is this new world concerned with socializations of this life. The world of earth life socializations and DNA is Law driven. We must keep in mind that strident Cosmic Laws drive Karma associated with these dynamics. Gurdjieff explains all of this in his wordy way and it is not so easy to fathom the gist of the whole process. What's more, unseen radiations are beamed into us in waves based on what has been earned. The invisible radiations are subject to change when active reasoning **overcomes** the script that dictates behavior and health of a human. It is worthwhile to ponder these profound ideas and to embrace—that is to live with understanding, work and intent to overcome negative or unsavory radiations.

A few years ago, one of my Tai Chi teachers, who appropriately showed little emotion while demonstrating the movements, remarked to me in a mode of utter amazement that he had seen on the History 2 channel, the strong suggestion that we humans were engineered by aliens. That was shocker for him as was the mention that some UFO craft have been spotted on earth, even now. My teacher was visibly troubled by what he had seen and heard and had difficulty processing the whole idea of more intelligent beings from other planets visiting earth. Clearly, we have come a long way in our understanding since Erich Von Daniken's book and the film known as **Chariots of the Gods** which suggest that aliens were here, have returned many times and had a hand in human engineering. Actually a trail of evidence was left behind that this is the case, it cannot be ignored by the inquisitive, the alert. One has only to visit the Egyptian exhibits at the Metropolitan Museum in New York, other major museums or to seriously ponder the writings of Zecharia Sitchin such as **"The Lost Realms"** to expand the mind toward fuller evidence. Lately, a bevy of other sages on the topic interviewed on the Coast to Coast radio talk show have provided insight which really is not too far afield, if we consider these notions carefully and ponder the evidence with objectivity. The Egyptian Master said to have worked with Elizabeth Haich also gives ample evidence when he describes the "Sons of God," a race of beings very different from humans who possessed "divine purity and existed without physical appetites, urges and passions which cast shadows on spirit."[116]

As much as it pains us to consider the concept that we humans were engineered by aliens or extraterrestrials—beings from other planets—we can give credit to Chris Hardy, Jim Marrs, Zecharia Sitchin and Von Daniken who are sages pointing to the same fact. There is ample evidence that there is life on other planets and at least some of it is vibrationally more intelligent than humans. This superior intelligence enables significant pursuits such as human cloning and technological sophistication beyond average human comprehension.[117] Those with closed minds have difficulty with this notion.

Chris Hardy, the author of **DNA *of the* Gods** aids us in understanding the scope and depth of human engineering. Capitalizing on the work of Zecharia Sitchin, Hardy reminds us that our DNA comes from alien sources, who engineered us "by blending their own divine DNA, that of Anunnaki Gods—the ones who had come down from Heaven to Earth with the DNA of an evolved ape-woman." Pay attention to Hardy's choice of the word "divine" for we'll get back to that word and the meaning associated with it. Our creation took place following extreme scientific experiments and some authorities say this tampering and tweaking continues until the present day. Many related dynamics were related to the process of jump starting the human race. For instance, we are advised by Hardy that certain important plants were brought from Nibiru the planet of origin of the Anunnaki and that wine was introduced as part of the human diet by these creator beings.[118] Not surprisingly, humans were fixed so as **not** to be more intelligent than our makers. In fact, it is clear that most of us were dumbed down and genetically flawed, although there is real genius among us, probably as a result of slip ups in engineering. What can we deduce from this? Well, obviously smarter, more dynamic humans are intellectually closer to the aliens that engineered us and others are closer to some of the animals used as part of the engineering process which took many years to perfect. A lot of us are in the middle. Gurdjieff's writings cleverly support this and we'll get to that very shortly. Clay tablets, numerous cave drawings and writings and now even big screen movies help us to grasp the evidence of this intricate programming and engineering—thus when we ask the "why" were we put here in the first place to live, suffer and die, it's not difficult to conclude that we were engineered initially to be slaves, underlings to the beings from far off who created us on earth. It is not far-fetched that they were simply experimenting; the same kind of experiments are being done today. Animal cloning and trafficking of human organs is now widely reported in magazines and journals. According to Hardy, we credit Ninmah, a genius of superior mind and instincts with creating genoms of the first evolved earth humans many thousands of years ago. It seems a curious fact that authors such as Mary Shelley and Mikhail Bulgakov created poignant stories of fiction about cloning, organ manipulation and human engineering many, many decades ago. Shelley's creation of "Frankenstein" in Great Britain in 1818 and Russian writer, Bulgakov's creation of "Heart of a Dog" in 1925 suggest that ideas about human engineering have been lurking for over 200 years and obviously longer. Both stories have survived the test of time and have been translated, filmed and studied all over the globe. In recent times, researchers such as Hardy, Marrs, Sitchen and Von Daniken have provided undeniably keen insight backed by evidence for contemporary humans to ponder. Now news about cloning, stem cell usage and organ transplants is part and parcel of medical science. How did ideas about all of this reach the human mind?

What makes sense, at least for me, is that some of us do behave like animals—always on the hunt, self-serving, a bit vicious, violent, war mongering and/or with really strange psychological cravings and practices. As a point of fact, one has only to read and watch mass media widely to see that some of us behave worse than some animals—even when there's no threat to necessitate such. Conversely, a few of us seem to be made of higher fabric—intelligent, responsible and intuitive, perhaps closer to the demi-gods who engineered us who had extraordinary powers, insight and the abilities such as astral travel, remote viewing, psychokinetic powers and other very superior attributes. We can all see flukes, structural snafus in the human system—strange mental and physical diseases and conversely unusual genius in all races in all epochs, throughout the globe. From whence do such mishaps and real genius originate? After all, medical science has shown us that DNA is clearly encoded, even I-Ching masters know this. We arrive from the womb with scripting! Some call this fate. Case studies have shown that scripting is even part of our organs, most especially the heart which holds on to information, even when transplanted into a new body.[119] Remarkably, if we comprehend what Gurdjieff intended and what is possible for humans following intensive Work and incarnations, it is possible to slowly dig out of the programming and perhaps even achieve longevity in the process. The essential point is Gurdjieff left behind a model for beginning the long process of overcoming our internal DNA and also external programming as well. This is not to say he could or would make it easy to accomplish this individual journey toward purity, away from Karma. But leave guideposts and methods to begin the process, he remarkably did.

In *Beelzebub's Tales*, Gurdjieff unfolds the notion of the link of extraterrestrials to human existence using metaphors and allegories—he hints that we were engineered from beings, led by a "Most High Commission" from a far off planet. It has been disconcerting for me to process all of these notions too, but the trail of evidence is remarkable and clear. It actually makes sense that there are other more intelligent beings in the universe. The age-old questions asked by the sages and intelligent humans still abound: "who are we?" "why are we here?" and is there any way to escape the earth prison?" In Chapter 10, "Why Men Are Not Men," of the book commonly known as the *Tales,* Gurdjieff reminds us of our "mechanical instinct" and how the beings that created us were ever fearful that we might act up and destroy the planet as we destroy ourselves and each other.[120] (*We seem to be doing exactly that most of the time, if we ponder the daily news political exploits, gang violence, disease and destruction. Humans have proclivities toward mayhem and unkindness toward each other; to boot, we are indeed greedy, war-like and have sexual aggression and other obsessive issues as well*). To press this point cogently, if humans are overly emotional, have violent tendencies toward war and conflict and regularly participate in practices harmful to themselves and to the earth which is alive with energy, then we need to be carefully monitored both by police on earth and from afar too. We should not have easy access to or possess any kind of substantial power because history teaches us that we will most likely abuse such a privilege. Our news sources are full of evidence of our abuses. Thus, we can deduce that our makers were obviously pretty smart—they knew how to clone, to manipulate us to have mostly scant knowledge and understanding—they opened our so-called minds to access just enough for us to get by—for the species to survive. They even engineered a fairly convenient way for us to procreate and attached emotions to the process. It seems obvious that the best way to supervise us—to keep humans under control and at the same time keep us divided and at each other's throats was to engineer diverse religions and attendant dogma first, followed by surveillance and cosmic monitoring systems. If ancient history is a good teacher, it would seem that humans have massively self destructed and probably had help from outside doing do, more than a couple of times. Evidence is now widespread for the intelligently-observant to ponder. Following human engineering, it was then necessary to keep us stepped down spiritually and this was done via the blood. In order to bring Spirit into the blood, real Work toward balance, harmony and overcoming programming, beyond what we are taught by mainstream religions has to become part and parcel of our being. We must be self-rewired—what the Christians have conveniently called, be born again into to a pure, light-filled mode. Christianity relays this important fact to us, but not clearly. In Tibetan traditions, this concept is referred to as "enlightenment of Buddhahood" and the idea is akin to Christianity: reprogram, die to the old self! Humans who want to rise up must reinvent themselves and that's not easy, but a few have accomplished it. But what does all of this mean? Ultimately, again, it means overcome programming!

With regard to the other worldly or extraterrestrial connection to human engineering, there has been still more evidence. All over the earth there exists undeniably perfectly formulated landing sites, pyramids and other laser sharp, practically indestructible structures which pre-date recorded history. All of this defies what we know of ancient technology. Hieroglyphs which pre-date our comfortable historical continuum also exist. This trail has been veiled and difficult to get at both in Gurdjieff's writings and in various versions of the Christian gospels, but it does exist. Those who have begun to understand hidden aspects of human existence intently, ponder the artifacts of antiquity from museum exhibits and develop their own intuitive instincts. Most of us seem not to want to know the real story of human creation and are comfortably mired in religious dogma that sometimes frankly does not make sense. Although written in a style not intended for the masses, Gurdjieff's own words are instructive about what he calls "biped three-brained beings" otherwise known as humans. For me, what he explains makes perfect sense as to why so much of the alien connection to human existence has been hidden, or shall we say veiled and lied about, over vast periods of time:

> **"The sacred members of this Most High Commission...reasoned that if the said mechanical instinct in the biped three-brained beings of that planet should develop towards the attainment of Objective Reason—as usually occurs everywhere among three-brained beings— then it might quite possibly happen that they would prematurely comprehend the real cause of their arising and existence and make a great deal of trouble..."[121]**

Gurdjieff says more about this in *Beelzebub's Tales*... For example, on page 149 he reminds us that "three brained beings" similar to humans breed on planets other than the earth and chiefs "exist also on all other planets" but are differently named—only our planet is unique because we have a "separate king for every accidentally segregated group and "sometimes several" chiefs. How did humans catch on so fast to a hierarchical structure that has been implemented in practically every aspect of human life, including cooperate, government, military, church and religion, families, mafia, medicine and higher education—even ghetto gangs have a tiered structure?

In Gnostic teachings, about which Gurdjieff knew and understood apparently a lot, comes the strident, numinous concept "Okidanokh," that is not so apparent in Christianity, Islamic or other world religions. But those who venture into real understanding, study religious traditions that are not native to them so as to cross reference the nectar of Divine messages not intended for the masses and of course to weed out the dross. In its full manifestation, the term has to do with an unseen but powerful equalizing cosmic substance that is available to humans who strive for perfection, purity and perfect harmonious balance. This substance is likely synonymous with "firmament" in the Christian Bible and is said to be God's gift connected to light and "Heaven" in Book of Genesis. The beginning of Paradise. OAHSPE also mentions this firmament substance in the Book of Openta-Armij which explains rather cogently "there are two things only in all the universe: the unseen firmament and the corporeal worlds that float therein."[122] The translation of this passage is clear to me—crossing over from the material or corporeal world to be coated by this cosmic substance or firmament is tantamount to the start of everlasting or eternal life. The select few who want this substance rendered to them have generally done no harm to others and work sincerely for harmony on earth planet and oneness with the Source. Atonement for egregious, awful stuff done previously is more or less possible, again, only for those who purely repent, see their errors and work off earlier unsavory behaviors through unselfish service to humanity. This does not happen in one life time. Planetary service is an important component to achieving oneness through Okidanokh. Strangely, a person cannot seek this cosmic substance or achieve it in artificial ways; it finds you or more cogently comes to some or is awarded as an unimaginable gift to a select few on an individual basis. This process cannot be facilitated for a person by some other human, it has to be achieved individually. Ministers and gurus cannot accomplish the process on your behalf. And, it's mind blowing to learn that this cosmic substance is revered by beings on other neighboring planets.[123] Thus, whether we achieve it or not does have an impact on beings existing on other neighboring planets. For those who have a difficult time with this notion, just imagine a neighbor who has a major sewage problem who lives next door or near you, or who has a tremendous flood on his property or who raises pigs in the backyard. Or imagine the damage done by atomic blasts, fracking, or murder and mayhem. All of this can and does effect us here but also surprisingly the earth's planetary neighbors in a very negative vibrational way. Even loud noises, bad smells, or so called "nasty" neighbors can have an exceedingly negative impact on quality of life for others. Likewise, kind, considerate, helpful neighbors are to be revered. To put an even sharper point on the notion of harmony, Okidanokh, as mentioned earlier, continues to be unimaginable for most of us, as it denotes a cosmic substance orchestrated and gifted by the Source, under the right, pure circumstances on a very individual basis. It should be stressed, this substance cannot be purchased, bargained for or negotiated. It is a supreme, Divine protective gift granted to those who strive to live in harmony and/or who strive for it in such an intensely graceful, pure way that the Source takes note and gifts it. Okidanokh cannot even be seen by scientists who have smart instruments. This extraordinary substance, made possible only by the Source, could be likened to the ultimate gift of the Holy Spirit and cannot be seen under a microscope, but in rare instances some humans have been known to "see" this rendering, when the veil is lifted.

It is instructive and beneficial to serious seekers, when similar conclusions are drawn from vastly different researchers and teachers, using diverse research methods. Deep meditation is essential. Ocke de Boer, the author of **Higher Being Bodies**, also writes much about the process of rising up, toward the shift in consciousness. He seems to say that rather than so much emphasis on this material body of ours, we ought to give attention to the Kesdjan body which is composed of stuff from our solar system. This stuff, once again, is Okidanokh. Here we ought to take keen note of the term solar system. Unseen by the naked eye, a coating of the chakras takes place as we begin to rise up, over life times. Ocke explains this process in Part 1 of his book, and reminds us cogently that it takes life times of Work before we begin to rise up.[124] Ocke apparently understood what Gurdjieff was trying to tell us and also what I have been shown psychically. Once again it should be repeated, the "coating" process with this unseen substance is something that most of us cannot imagine. It is a difficult and tricky process indeed, for the obvious reason that we bump up against other people where ever we live on earth who don't have a clue about the necessity to work on themselves. Distortions prevail. The process gets more complicated because some humans are born with very superior gifts of insight and intuition, even healing powers, but that doesn't always mean that they are really "higher being bodies." Ocke de Boer reminds that as we get closer to the Source, changes take place in the chakras. And, I've come to understand that more significant changes also take place in the blood. Here, we pay special attention to the blood in connection with a shift in consciousness and the rose is symbolic of what takes place in the blood—a well veiled fact for thousands of years. Gurdjieff's hints in several passages from *Beelzebub's Tales to His Grandson* that "Roses, Roses" are connected to "Paradise" and later in the book, he connects roses to what most humans refer to as "GOD." [125]

So, how did Gurdjieff make the connection of a corresponding change in the blood of an aspirant when a shift in consciousness occurs? From numerous books and films about him and the man's own writings, we can all glean bits of Gurdjieff's biography, but little is known about his inner world, except from those very close to him and those who have seriously studied and been guided by the writings he left behind. Of Greek and Armenian descent, he travelled widely for most of his adult life as he sought answers to deep questions about the nature of man and the quest to rise up toward a shift in consciousness. With time and dedicated effort, surely Gurdjieff's intuition grew as did his spiritual powers. This is possible when one is purely on the path, over lifetimes. Offered here is educated conjecture coupled with keen intuition, but there exists also a trail in perennial literature that I've studied for more than a decade, across four continents.

And so, we might then ponder a link to Sufism since it is undeniably an aspect of the Gurdjieff teachings, as is Gnosticism or esoteric Christianity. A 12th century poet, Farid UD-Din Attar, provides us with incredible insight, in the spirit of the Persian poet Rumi, through intelligent, clever and highly metaphysical prose and verse. Attar wrote a series of poems and stories known as *The Conference of the Birds,* a classic in the Sufi tradition. A sample of it will be instructive here. Early in the series of poems and essays Attar acquaints us with the importance of giving up the ego self in order to rise up. In quick summary about the book of stories and verses, many birds have come together to have their say in a united nations styled summit, in preparation to know the Divine. But immediately, complaints begin, excuses not to make the journey abound from a variety of birds. Classic is the nightingale's profound plea that he can't really make the journey because he's love sick. Says the nightingale, "I'm so drowned in love that I find no thought of my existence in my mind. Her worship is sufficient life for me." Other birds chime in with excuses, but one who knows better than the nightingale says "My love is for the rose; I bow to her; From her dear presence I could never stir." [126] The mysterious man who appears in the poem explains that the rose "flowers" for him; her buds are for him and he wouldn't leave her, not even for a night. And a little known mythical bird called the hoopoe also responds to the nightingale's timid response regarding the journey to know the Divine. Says the hoopoe to the nightingale, "superficial love which makes you quail is only for outward show of things, renounce the delusion and prepare your wings." [127] Few of us it seems have this strident kind of resolve regarding our quest for a shift in consciousness. We're having problems getting our wings to fly! To boot, sometimes it seems the case that our attachment to religious traditions, political camps, domestic ups and downs actually stand in the way of the quest; there is also the problem of making a living—"putting bread on the table" to use a common expression. All of this can and does get in the way of flight. Highest teachings say nothing ought stand in the way.

Gurdjieff reminds us that "a man who does not possess his own world" (good self mastery and balance) can never do anything from his own initiative: all actions "are done" in him. Essentially Gurdjieff seems to be telling us that we're being controlled and manipulated from elsewhere, until we learn to manage ourselves, which most of us have difficulty DOING. He says more about this in **Life is Real Only, Then, When I Am:** we can receive help, if the intent is pure and we struggle with doing Work on ourselves."[128] This particular book, said to be Gurdjieff's most esoteric, must be read and studied carefully multiple times and if the reader's level of Being is right, certain vibrational responses occur. This is extraordinary and no talk or missive can adequately explain it. Something in the blood changes when we arrive at a shift in consciousness; it pours in from elsewhere. But this fact has apparently been carefully guarded although hinted at by various Christian religious traditions. The process has been little understood, so much misunderstood in fact that really crazy, misguided humans do all sorts of rituals connected with the blood, including animal and even human sacrifices. Humans have always suspected there was something special about the blood, that there was a connection to God or higher consciousness in some way. When the fragrant beauty of the rose is considered thoughtfully and with full attention, it is so obvious that there's something extra special about it. The spirals of the red rose symbolize the unseen changes that take place in the blood when one comes to transformation and is on a pure quest for eternal life. This is the reason, it seems to me, that Gurdjieff associates the rose with paradise on page, 217 in what is commonly known by Gurdjieff's students as the *Tales*. He doesn't spell this out for us per se, but he hints at it and requires us, as the Bible does in its numerous mentions, to understand that blood is the key to atonement. But the process has been misunderstood by heathens and Christians alike globally. Heathens have often resorted to animal and even human sacrifice, realizing that there's something extraordinary they're supposed to do regarding blood to get closer to redemption and what they perceive as God.

Of course, sadly, they miss the boat! In **Beelzebub's Tales,** the revered *Emerald Tablets are mentioned by the code name "marble tablets"*[129] *but in the chapter "Ashiata Shiemash Sent to Earth" the blood connection is made clear.*

The Emerald Tablets are amazing as they explain cogently how to achieve eternal life and how to avoid the halls of death. It is said in Egyptian mythology that great pains were taken to keep *The Emerald Tablets* away from human beings, especially the profane. They were well hidden from humans, buried deeply in several places on earth as explained in an earlier chapter. Nevertheless Gurdjieff says because of this being-character that he names Ashiata Shiemash in the *Tales* required it. Moreover he explains "At the present time this surviving tablet is the chief sacred relic of a small group of initiated beings" referred to as the Brotherhood-Olbogmek. We are made to understand that Ashiata did not teach anything to "ordinary three-brained beings of the earth, nor did he preach anything to them, as was done before and after him by all the Messengers sent there from above..."[130] The Very Saintly Ashiata Shiemash was careful to leave his teachings to a small group of initiates to be "transmitted from generation to generation." The Brotherhood referred to here, it seems to me, is most likely The Brotherhood of the White Temple which operates fully today for those who seek it out and patiently wade through the lessons in order to understand the workings of the universe and the human condition and the meaning of death. *The Emerald Tablets* make it clear that the blood changes once there has been a shift in consciousness, this is a prime aspect of initiation. In Tablet XII, titled "*the Secret of Secrets*," we are taught that only through significant effort is eternal life possible, and we must each break the "fetter of darkness which binds" us to the sphere of earth.[131] We are three natured, physical, mental and astral according to the *Tablets* but most of us never come to know the astral quality. Calmness of the mind and other work is necessary to prepare. Then, when the right time comes, the blood moves in a vortical motion which has been referred to as "etherization" a process that is reserved for adepts and initiates.[132] The clincher is this: none of us can make it happen; it is undoubtedly a gift from the Divine which is given only when we are perceived to be ready.

Thus, we can conclude that the red rose symbolizes a change in the blood, which begins to move, in a mimic of the spiraling rose petals. Doing the Work, not debating it or intellectualizing it, opens the door to stop internal and external programming. Eventually a shift in the blood occurs and this is signified in the intense spirals of the red roses. This understanding was so profound that Gurdjieff simply stopped writing after he uncovered it, perhaps with the thought that those of us who could get it, would get it and others would have to wait and do more Work to fathom the gist and heart of it. It is a profoundly esoteric message. If we can completely quiet the mind, go into complete retreat from the sense-driven world again, and again and again, over long periods, something begins to happen that is beyond words, beyond thought—there is an unseen change in the blood that medical science seemingly knows nothing about. We're simply lifted into higher realms, the vibration is different in this realm as Gurdjieff tells us cogently and it is in this state that the blood, unseen, by medical science, can change, into a vortex-like movement that mimics the Source of creation and is in fact connected to it. Simply put, we create a "new world" to use Mr. Gurdjieff's term and he reminds us cogently on page 173 of **Life is Real** that "A Man who does not possess his own world can never do anything from his own initiative: again, it should be underscored, all his actions "are done" in him." In fact, a few of us who've made the trek through reading, re-reading and understanding *Life is Real* several times, know that it is a magical book; again, the most esoteric and profound instruction of Gurdjieff's writings.

Now, in case more evidence is needed that the blood is the bridge to the Holy Spirit and that changes take place in the blood of humans once the pure, right link has been made, the work of two other astute researchers, writing from differing perspectives and at widely different time periods is instructive. First, Trevor Ravenscroft's writing about the blood from the timeless work known as *The Spear of Destiny,* copywritten initially in 1973 by the estate of Ravenscroft provides remarkable insight. An unusual and obviously brilliant man himself, Ravenscroft sought out a teacher, Dr. Walter Johannes Stein in order to better understand a mysterious spear's connection to the story of the crucifixion and the Nazi connection to it. The Vienna-born Dr. Stein was a doctor of philosophy, intuitive of superior powers, and as well had been advisor to Winston Churchill regarding the psychological underpinning of the Nazi operation during World War II. Some of the top Nazi leaders dabbled in metaphysics and were active in the occult world, to say the least. Stein told Ravenscroft of his own out of body experience during WWI on the battle front in 1914, in which "he came to the conclusion that, because he was intent on reaching a kind of thinking no longer dependent on the brain, the content of his meditation should be of a sense free nature… He chose the ancient Rosicrucian meditation on the Black Cross and the Seven Red Roses."[133] From his meditation practices, Stein came to understand and embrace the inner significance of the blood, the central theme of the search for the [Holy] Grail. Thus, it was in the midst of a WWI battlefield that Stein came to understand the connection of the blood to the Holy Spirit.

There is even more recent, further testimony and explanation of the potential connection of the human blood to higher consciousness or what is commonly referred to as the *Holy Spirit*. Christopher Vesey, a Swiss naturopath specializing in detoxification and rejuvenation is the author of many books and has practiced widely. Thus Vesey's academic background and interests are far different from Ravenscroft's. And yet both men from vastly differing experiences, one a World War, battlefield soldier and academic researcher of a mysterious spear, and the other from a naturopathic-scientific perspective, reached the same conclusion. Vasey's book, *The Spiritual Mysteries of Blood*, is a masterpiece in that it is simple to read and easy to comprehend; it makes the clear blockbuster connection of the blood to higher realms.

As mentioned earlier, the gospels hint at this but ministers in the Christian tradition seem to know only part of the story or at least it's never fully explained in various sermons I've heard widely and regularly at services in numerous locales. Humans grow up hearing there is something about the blood that "saves" us and have sipped symbolic wine or grape juice from many a chalice, signifying the blood of Christ, but the process goes largely unexplained. Vesey does a better job of explaining the internal process than any sermon I've ever heard. He writes: "The raison d'etre of the blood is therefore to serve the spirit. The blood has to be present to form the bridge for the spirit to incarnate into the physical body." Moreover, and this is profound, Vesey makes it clear that the spirit is connected to the blood and "only through the blood does it then connect to the body." As I suspected long ago and Gurdjieff's teachings made extraordinarily clear, this is not an automatic process. This and only this, is the key to eternal life. Light filled Work must be accomplished for this unseen, miraculous process to take place on a highly selective and individual basis, apparently over life times. The Essence of the SOURCE reaches us only when we gracefully purify ourselves and are ready to stop being slaves to the world of the senses. When he died in 1949, Gurdjieff left behind the supreme gift of a system or method of how to begin the process of introducing higher vibration, higher consciousness into body. The thing that sets his teachings in a singular class is that the Work he designed and proffered is to be accomplished while at the same time, we are out on the streets and byways of life. Put another way, those involved in the Gurdjieff tradition do not shut away in monasteries, ashrams or long-term retreats away from it all; the mission is more difficult: to work first toward being good householders, to serve when possible while at the same time doing personal, practical, light-filled Work on the SELF.

An urgent summary about Okidanokh: it is a prime rendering from the Source like none other. But, according to Gurdjieff in Chapter 39 of the *Tales*, there are hundreds of other substances in seven classes or radiations which also shower humans. These substances pour into and around us based on our quality of being—that is based on our vibratory states which are subject to change. These intricate processes are unseen and mostly imperceptible except for a select few for whom the veil has been lifted. It is therefore more urgent than we ever imagined, to live harmonious lives, free from grief, anger, despair, and so on. Working harder to avoid extreme emotions and judgements is essential for those of us who truly understand the human predicament.

Chapter Five

"Spectre of a Rose..."
Validations of Gurdjieff's
Last Teaching

To summon the spectre of a Rose

We cannot revive old factions

We cannot restore old policies

Or follow an antique drum...

Accept the constitution of silence

From T.S. Eliot, Four Quartets

In a remarkable effort to reach a small group of humans who tried again and again to make otherworldly contact, in the early 1980s a super extraterrestrial being adjusted its frequency in order to respond. The being identified as RA was reported to have transmitted the following urgent notice to the group based in Kentucky, United States: "We are those who are of the Law of One. In our vibration the polarities are harmonized; the complexities are simplified; the paradoxes have a solution..."[134] The interpretation of this important message was clear: humans need to learn to avoid conflict, harmonize and seek balance in all matters. This is the essential foundation to higher consciousness, to overcoming the sense-driven world where things are done to humans based on past life Karma transmitted into the mind and body usually with DNA distortions. This karmic inpouring was called "internal programming" by Gurdjieff and it is now acknowledged and verified through medical science that certain traits, illnesses and so on are encoded to DNA. The information on how our health and mental states will take shape follows a script that comes in from elsewhere; it is born into us from inception. Master astrologers and high level intuitives seem to have understood this fact before medical science could catch up enough to write the theory associated with the process.[135] The script comes in as a result of our behaviors, as recorded in a cosmic record that has been labeled Karma.

There is also another process that usually plagues humans, the conditioned-programming of this life on earth dictated by socio-economic status, education level, religious dogma, mass media, traumas, geographic birth place, dietary choices and so on and on—this is known as "external programming." Obviously the two processes are interrelated; they work in tandem. When overdone with distortions, the external programming is as potentially detrimental to a human's quest for higher consciousness as the internal programming that comes from the karmic record. Our mission, if we choose to accept it, is to navigate adroitly around both programs. Gurdjieff was well aware of these important revelations and he is not the only one who tried to alert humans that this was our plight. Over vast spans of time, in almost every epoch, astute teachers and mystics have been on earth to teach us the way out of the human quagmire. Whereas others have quietly revealed the situation in a variety of written and veiled ways, Gurdjieff, as mentioned in the last chapter, was indeed unique in leaving behind a method or system of how to overcome both internal and external programming. He imparted the plan to select humans in a somewhat unusual manner involving group work, exotic dance movements, full attention to self observation without harsh judgments, sitting meditations and most important, a practice known as Self Remembering.

The method Gurdjieff left behind is guarded and considered sacred by groups that embrace it globally, most likely to shield it from adulteration by those who do not understand it in the purest of light. Also, Gurdjieff's teachings and methods are shielded and provided in dribbles to those who stay the course as is most esoteric work. Bits and pieces of important lessons are provided slowly apparently so as to leave ultimate benefits exclusively for those who can wake up—or, as has been said, who "have eyes to see." Thus, the explicit message of RA in the 1980s and of other superior beings have been ever present but elusive from the masses: WORK toward, try diligently for balance of emotion and polarity in order to rise up. Like RA's attempts to communicate with a small group, deep teaching of what humans ought to Work on has been ever provided by obviously "selected" individuals and provided to us in parables, allegories, poetry, and great literature as we have witnessed in the preceding essays. The paragon message is the need for humans to find balance, in order to overcome suffering during earth life and beyond. We are reminded in numerous ways that it is essential to "cool It," to relax naturally in meditation and to Work toward elevating frequencies toward the vertical life, as exemplified by the upward plank of the cross symbol in Christianity.

This essay explores from a variety of sources this most essential message ever given to humans. It also serves as exquisite, diverse validation of Gurdjieff's last teaching in *Life Is Real Only Then, When "I Am."*

While in New York City in the Spring of 1935, Gurdjieff was having a particularly restless night revolving around writing of the last portion of his final book. During the early morning hours, he strolled the City's streets and pondered ideas he intended to convey until finally he broke the thinking process about his essay long enough to purchase a newspaper in the Russian language, *Russky Golos*, (Russian Voice) dated April 14, 1935. The front page missive that grabbed his attention was on the subject of longevity and was written by Metchnikov who drew the conclusion that where very old people are concerned, if they are very active and mobile, healthy and appeared not to look their age, it is likely that their blood was often like that of a young person.

Here again we are reminded of the real urgency of harmonizing and balancing polarity and especially the emotions. Subsequently the blood follows in this balancing process which, it must be underscored, is the reason for so much hoop la about the blood in religious traditions globally. Emotional balance comes first and is the corollary to other balancing—that is in diet, drinking the right water, Ph levels and overall polarity. The goal of course now and evermore is to also achieve what Gurdjieff called an "intentional blending" or rising out of both inner and outer programming. A hard ask. But a simple example to press the point might be edifying. Suppose you are born with the proclivity to worry or to be overweight or to steal from others or to do anything else that is spiritually detrimental. If you can free-willfully overcome vices such as these or other distortions—really SEE yourself,—then your DNA adjusts so that later on or in a subsequent life, this is one thing you will not have to "pay for" or live through again in the karmic sense. There is a demerit system in place that we cannot see, although some of us are aware of it as we can indeed see vast suffering of humans on earth. Unless you have had an astute past life regression done, it is likely that you have no idea what you are paying for or why you are suffering to whatever extent in this life. Some people do know what they are paying for and why their particular suffering is taking place. I've had the good fortune to have met a couple of these people and they understand how and why they must serve to offset "bad" Karma from previous incarnations. In other words, they have been fortunate to understand the karmic process enough to take right actions to correct past egregious or snotty behaviors. This suffering dynamic has been discussed widely in the book, *The Tibetan Book of the Dead* which is little known in the West. The book explains that a few "psychonauts," that is selected human voyagers have been permitted to see or recall their past lives and the acts that have hampered their growth in a particular incarnation. And so it is, these special humans are granted heightened opportunity to self-correct and to fix any unsavory behaviors because they have been awarded snapshots of themselves from the past.[136] This obviously is not tied to luck.

The process of all of this is intricate and involved, but everything is recorded in what has been called the Universal Mind which is one of the first intransgressible Cosmic Laws. These Laws, it should be reminded, **cannot** be broken. This message has been available to us for hundreds, even thousands of years, but few humans seem to be aware of what they mean or the consequences of not working in harmony with the Laws. The result of heeding the messages should be obvious; if we can achieve balance and keep out of trouble it is possible to eventually get off the wheel—the plague of a most profound karmic Law, *cause and effect*. Why? Because in balance, we don't set up bad or negative Karma for ourselves. And, as astute teachers, top tier astrologers and especially masters of the Chinese I-Ching have reminded us, we are under planetary influences which operate in tandem with Karma in a script or code into individual DNA—that is to say we must be liberated from the spheres of planetary forces in order to rise up. In a masterfully esoteric essay written for **Quest,** *the* magazine of the Theosophical Society, Richard Smoley traced the mystery of the seven seals and reminds us that an initiate, an evolved human, who can manage over lifetimes to achieve balance "reaches a level of consciousness and being that is above the domain of the planets."[137] Pure freedom. To underscore the essential point here: our endeavor ought to be to overcome planetary forces.

In this quest for freedom from suffering and to achieve what some religious denominations call the "eternal life" of the Masters, we might do well to ponder this short 12th

century verse "A Madman seeks Shelter" from Farid Ud Din
Attar's *The Conference of the Birds*[138]:

> "A naked madman, gnawed by hunger, went
> Along the road—his shivering frame was
>   bent
> Beneath the icy sleet; no house stood there
> To offer shelter from the wintry air.
> He saw a ruined hut and with a dash
> Stood underneath its roof; a sudden crash
> Rang out—a tile had fallen on his head,
> And how the gaping gash it cut there bled!
> He looked up at the sky and yelled: "Enough!
> Why can't you clobber me with better stuff?"

Anyone who has consulted a really efficient astrologer
has at least some sense of being jerked around by planetary
forces which, like a finely tuned clock, ultimately give back
the reap that we have sown. The naked madman in the verse
was simply getting back from the Universal Mind, that grand
omnipotent recorder of suffering and all else, exactly what he
had previously put into the pool. For the observant, it is obvi-

ous that the most egregious—those who do harm to themselves and others will be held back and very likely will experience more and more suffering, to be meted out in various lifetimes, until such time there is an awakening to the process. Stridently mean humans who fail to overcome their heinous behaviors over lifetimes may actually get kicked out of the human kingdom altogether. A serious, just God operating here is easy to imagine. The meting out process is apparently not sure to happen exactly in one lifetime. Harm done in previous lifetimes catches up, remarkably. Those who have consulted masters of the *I-Ching* come away with a strong sense that something or someone out there knows what is going to occur long before it happens. In history there are many documented examples of this.

We are orchestrated, based on past life Karma; we generally get what we deserve, one way or the other, sooner or later. The *I-Ching* is perhaps little known in the West, but it is one of the oldest, if not the oldest oracle book on earth. To Dr. Martin Schonberger's credit, he has enlightened us that the *I-Ching* is tied to the genetic code and medical science now realizes the coding comes in from elsewhere and determines much about who we are, our level of health and longevity and more. Described by a Tibetan Lama as a "psychic computer," the phenomenal *I-Ching* unfolds our script "provided by Nature in the form of the genetic code, and may thus be conceived as a programming of the fate of each living creature." [139] Remarkably, in highly unusual leadership, what Gurdjieff taught was a slow method of overcoming the script. How can humans be convinced to overcome staunch personalities and egos that propel them? Most of us do not even realize this is a desirable goal. The mission is to become one with the Source, not to be flung out doing the wild and crazy stuff that humans do so well. Murder, theft, greed, warmongering, personal judging and other ills seem to abound as part and parcel of the human condition. To free ourselves from being jerked around by the imprint awarded us at the time of conception and embedded into the DNA code, we are required to do a lot of good, balanced Work. The aim is to Work our way back to the Source, in the right fashion, that is with corrections and necessary balances. Many of us on earth have labeled the Source of all and everything "God" or the "Force," because we have not come up with better words or descriptions. Humans have also concocted all sorts of hidden or unspeakable names for God. An urgent saying of our time from science fiction movies is: may the "Force be with you." But this cannot happen without intense Work and service and an undying quest to do **no** harm—that is, in general, do not make matters worse here on earth. This important point is underscored in the teachings of Gurdjieff. He beseeches us to understand the audacity and karmic penalties associated with harming someone else, who in fact, is not our own creation or property. Here it is easy to make the analogy of someone unauthorized coming into your home to create havoc. That is effectively the damage done when we hurt others psychologically or physically. We must learn to tread lightly, to be careful and thoughtful in our words and treatment of others.

There is strident evidence to support Gurdjieff's teaching that we must overcome both internal and external programming. Eons ago, throughout the years and now, this has been a quiet but urgent message to humans intent on rising out of the DNA imprint and also earthly-driven socializations that are often detrimental. How can rising up be accomplished, if most of us are steeped in big or puny egos that keep us tripped up or in despair over one material thing or the other? Some of us are born with proclivities to cause upset to ourselves and others. DNA scripting can be very problematic for most of us it seems. Gurdjieff designed a system to help us dig out, but he did not remind us enough that most humans cannot in the ordinary sense "do" the necessary work. Some of us try and a few even think we can. Real help comes in from the Source in mysterious ways when the trying has been pure and continuous over long periods. Some of us refer to this as miracles. Tests are interwoven in the process. Gurdjieff never finished the last chapter of his final book *Life Is Real Only Then, When 'I Am'*. We wonder why? Did he realize that the vast majority of us cannot really change substantially in one incarnation, that we are destined to go on with the hard knocks of struggle and suffering, around and around over multiple life times? Was he able to see into the future far enough to know what is happening now: DNA hacking and tweaking? Does this latest DNA tampering and tweaking actually have a bearing on the spiritual process of ascension? I think not. The invisible Lords of Karma know all and are undoubtedly capable of adjusting to anything. I have personally witnessed this and been utterly amazed by it. So, my educated, intuitive hunch is that even when the system can be "tricked" in this realm by medical science, there are other realms and dimensions which cannot be controlled by tampering of humans. The Lords of Karma know how to override tampering of the human body, organs, and entire human system and the evidence is that they do when warranted.

Simply put, we have not been able to accomplish the "third world"—that middle world beyond the detrimental opposites that jerk us around. We drift through life and then croak. While on earth, mental, emotional conflict and all sorts of suffering is prevalent for most humans and this carries over into politics, religion and subsequently, almost perpetually, transmits vibrationally to troubled nations. Even when there are no massively big problems, a few so called leaders create them and pull the rest of us into a never-ending fray. Our so-called elected leaders are symbolic of the disfunction of humanity. Conflicted humans lead conflicted nations, both in a hurdle of disharmony that impacts all of us. We also manage to tear into and abuse the earth with the same ease with which we dig into and hurt each other. Obviously, and the evidence is widespread and mounting, most of us in some way are participants in a low, negative vibration of divisiveness. We seem to have some level of comfort in what the extraterrestrial RA termed our "distortion." [140] This distorted suffering is the lot of most humans. We over eat, over drink the wrong stuff, over spend, and to boot have attitudes to give our personalities more pop. We are easily swayed by various programs, like pressures to make children for whom we are not responsibly prepared to lead and teach. There are special humans who, after many years and past lives of quiet work and meditation, have overcome the proclivity of argument and divisiveness. But it is simply difficult to find a human organization where conflict or some level of tension does not exist.

In the most auspicious chapter of the final unfinished writing of Gurdjieff was revealed this truth: nothing really light filled and everlastingly good will happen for humans until this Work of overcoming programming, internal and external is done. Connected to this fact, profoundly, to say the least, is the book *Life Is Real Only Then, When 'I Am'*.[141] Gurdjieff's teaching in this little-known book was far reaching but not so cogently available for those outside the traditions that require quiet study, meditation and Work to achieve higher being. As has been explored in his other books, nothing on this planet is as we have been taught it to be, thus, George Ivanovich Gurdjieff again and again in a variety of teachings beseeched us to overcome inner programming (DNA encoded) and external programming (societal) in order to rise up to longevity on this planet and to a higher being spiritual life as well. Gurdjieff assures us of a couple of essential facts in pursuit of higher consciousness. First, when we operate in a closed mind with only our own views to guide us, we are held back. In order to overcome, to acquire "force of expansion," we must overcome—grow outside of ourselves, our religions, our opinions, judgements, etc. In doing so, we acquire a powerful vibratory quality which expands at a great, unseen, unimaginable distance. And, moreover, second, we must strive for a state of pure "complete relaxation" which also increases or enhances vibration. So, the Christians were apparently right about one important thing, although they mostly do not practice what has been taught: die to the old self in order to hope for the possibility of an eternal life. Big thoughts to ponder; big work to do; too big for most of us to even think about as we struggle to simply get through family and work stuff and to manage our ways around GMO's, global conflicts, and mundane stuff of earth planet life. Now we have also developed detrimental technological habits (more and better automatic weapons, over use of cell phones, computers, etc.) that seem to have overtaken humans in a kind of broad side assault.

Pay Close Attention to Words and Behavior

Yes! There seems a blockage, a dumbing-down of the vast majority of us. Could it be that something or someone does not want us to have easy access to the keys to eternal life, full ascension? From *The Emerald Tablets*, we are privy to the arch-essential message that drives the human kingdom. And although permission is not given to quote too much directly from the "Secret of Secrets" tablet number twelve here, a very brief overview will suffice for the well intended. It is advantageous to seek out the real *Tablets* and to study it intently and patiently. The true *Tablets* is a mysterious book which will not permit one to read or comprehend it completely until a heightened state of Being is achieved. It must be read and studied numerous times. In fact, tablet twelve explains the workings of the human body which tie it to a magnificent invisible energy; **the flow** of this energy must be kept in perfect balance at all times in order to achieve optimum growth toward higher consciousness and ultimately longevity. The key is the flow, it must be kept in optimum balance. Until we start real Work on ourselves to rise up, what flows in is a not-so-apparent detrimental "wave of vibration" that simply binds and keeps us attached to the senses. Like being in prison, we are bound to the tomb of the human body. We are also bound to matter, to the Karma of past lives, undoubtedly a cage of sorts. Moreover, unbelievably, this wave of vibration is so finely tuned and orchestrated by the Lords of Karma that it gives us back precisely what we have earned in this and previous lives, as legislated by unbreakable Cosmic Laws. Phenomenal stuff for sure. Cosmic Laws actually dictate how everything is meted out, justly and appropriately to every incarnation. Worth underscoring in light of the so called new attempts at cloning and organ transplants is that bad Karma will catch up to the rightful owner, even if it takes several life times to do so. Thus, an awful person who gets an organ transplant that extends his life this time, will have negative Karma folded in eventually, after death in the next or even far off lifetime. This is important to note since key organs such as heart and brain cart over scripting from previous owners. This has been well documented. Also, important to understand is that there is a hierarchy to the whole process; this is actually pretty obvious, except to the wild-west, "do as I please" types who do not and cannot understand that there are consequences for every-thing said, thought and done and, interestingly, to "intent" as well. In other words, things might not turn out well in certain situations of the life of a human, but the Lords of Karma inherently know and factor in the intent of the individual in all matters on earth. By the way, you cannot lie to them or trick them, even if you want to. No sincere good or harm done or nasty intent goes unrecorded. Added to all of this, it is a prime point to mention, we are not all on the same level. Ponder the hierarchy in practically everything on earth. All serious work forces from military, martial arts, police departments, firefighting professionals, elementary thru higher education, the corporate world and even so-called mafia and ghetto gangs operate in a hierarchical structure. All of these organizations operating globally are based on rank. Some type of reward is given at the time of moving up and likewise some form of discipline is often meted out for slip ups and wrong behaviors. Where and how did humans get the wherewithal to structure tiered systems in practically everything on earth? Is this a programmed-in, primordial ordering that we have simply fallen into? To press the point, please note that even the plant, mineral and animal worlds are hierarchical in structure. Some plants, for instance, are very poisonous and others have high vibration healing properties, ordained from elsewhere, that provide healing and when administered properly, can be lifesaving. The same tiered structure is true of the rock and mineral kingdom as well. A few rocks and crystals have healing properties, some are just there for the blasting. Heaven also has tiers or levels according to Dante's *Divine Comedy*: "in Paradise each soul is perfectly blessed, according to its capacity...there are even degrees of glory."[142] So, really smart people can grasp this and start immediately the slow process of digging out of the human quagmire. Paying close attention to one's words and behavior is just the beginning of shoveling out.

Additional validation of Gurdjieff's teachings and the path to higher consciousness that he wanted us to understand comes to us exquisitely from significant quarters, including magnificent poetry, art and even melodic classical, heavenly music as has been noted in a previous essay. Explore now, for instance, the message of essential balance in a somewhat obscure series of letters to a British journalist from the Mahatmas. So, who are the Mahatmas? For the unaware, unimaginably, there are ascended beings, a bevy of Masters who can take shape and appear when and where the need exists. They operate as aids to the Source and to the Lords of

Karma mostly from behind the scenes. In other words, the Masters are unseen and largely unknown to most humans. The only validation I can offer here is that it is clear to me intuitively that they exist. Plus, a lot of evidence has been provided in these essays. For those who have difficulty with the concept of ascended masters, simply consider what we've been taught of the life of Jesus. Everyone in the west knows at least something of his story. One of the many missions of these Masters is to tap and to guide seriously developing chelas and adepts. In the late 19ᵗʰ century an overly inquisitive British journalist named A. P. Sinnett let his strong desire to communicate with ascended Masters become known through Helena P. Blatvatsky (known as HPB to Theosophists). She had apparently mentioned the existence of the Mahatmas during her travels and teachings. Sinnett became eager for proof of their existence. A man for his time, Alfred Sinnett most assuredly had never encountered a woman like Blatvatsky; he had doubts about her motives and the mysterious things she said and did were quite likely foreign to him. Sinnett probably wanted initially to poke holes into HPB's accounts that she had been guided by otherworldly ascended beings who were said to have propelled her writings and aided her remotely to establish the Theosophical movement. She was also in regular communication with a Master. The Theosophical endeavor co-founded by HPB was and is an apparent alternative to various religions which have existed on earth for thousands of years, but have not adequately aided humans to overcome their divisive, violence-instigating nature. Organized religions—most denominations—plain and simply have not really on a large scale brought people together or taught us how to behave toward each other. Must we live with the threat of conflict, nuclear weapons and war looming, all the time? Strangely, we have figured a way to send chaplains of various denominations off to the front lines of wars which were not truly necessary in the first place. We pray, supposedly to God, and then fight to tear up someplace or something that we don't like to gain something desirable supposedly; after that, we egotistically reward certain soldiers for bravery. Later, past enemies become friends when it is economically advantageous. Then, amazingly, the whole process repeats at another time in another geographic location. Humans also proudly continue a pattern of proudly identifying with their religions almost as much as they do with their militaries. And we still hold on to divides that are historically deep and, I think, plain stupid. No proof of any of this is necessary for the observant and it is a global process.

So, to get back to the point of the start of the Theosophy movement and Alfred Sinnett, it was probably with the dual purpose of providing proof to him that the Mahatmas really existed and as a validation that HPB was honest in her claims about knowing them that the Masters entered into a rare correspondence. There may have been the residual aim of seizing an opportunity during the launch period of Theosophy to ostensibly work through a talented, respected and well known journalist like Sinnett who would be certain to get the word out in widely established channels of communication. For a brief while, the Mahatmas made themselves public so to speak and this inherently supported the Theosophical movement and HPB's work. Of course, most people did not read and still are not aware of the correspondence rendered by the Mahatmas.

And so, *The Mahatma Letters*, in book form was eventually published, numerous times from 1923 through the 1990s, under the auspices of the Theosophical University Press. As proof, particular messages inside the book authenticated the validity of the letters—that is inside the paragraphs is presented the inner most thoughts and actions of certain individuals in HBP's and Sinnett's community during the time. The diverse group of letters contain private discussions based on questions put to the Mahatmas directly from Sinnett. The descriptions and private thoughts of individuals put forth in the letters were not public at the time and were generally impossible to know, except by unseen Masters who could intercept human thought. The ultimate surveillance team. Actually, it is a little known fact, there are a few extraordinary humans among us now and in the past who can accomplish some of the same feats used by the Masters such as clairvoyance, clairaudience and psychokinetics. But we rarely know who they are, unless they want us to know. True Masters have these and other powers and they also know God in the sense that they have achieved eternal life. One of the Mahatma Masters explained why HPB appeared to be nervous and why she had quirks in temperament which many people in her circle had observed. The original letters are now housed at the London Museum. To study the letters is to become enriched in worlds beyond the average imagination and understanding. But there is also contained in the letters plenty of validation of the Law of cause and effect. Nothing happens by chance, a fact also well substantiated in *The Emerald Tablets*—which assures us of that mostly unknown ring of vibration around the earth which metes out exactly what a human deserves based on how that individual has lived, thought, and done to others. This process is as assured as the encoding of DNA. It just is and always has been since human existence as we know it. The sooner humans understand it and live significantly better, the sooner the ring of vibration will emit good vibration stuff to them. No guru, politician or prayer can change this meting out. Also, scary to know is that confessions to others of wrong doing or what we call sins mean practically nothing. We must each accomplish our own clean up and change. A famous monk-priest known as Martin Luther figured this out for himself in the 16th century when he got himself in trouble with the church for complaining about the practice known as indulgence—that is paying to have sins removed. What can mitigate, although not erase, our wrongdoing in the world of Karma is pure acknowledgment of wrong, solid repentance and some type of thoughtful, well intended work of reversal. Change or reversal is essential. This fusion dynamic helps to step down the negative vibration that the ill done has caused. Sometimes we hurt even ourselves; this too is a factor in

Karma. When looked at this way, we come to understand that all of our misdeeds work against Divine light energy and against ourselves in the long run of multiple incarnations. This is the reason to be careful about everything. Obviously, it is best to break ties with people who block pure light from your life and hang close to those who seem to emit it or open doors that let it flow in.

The Mahatma Letters do not dwell on polarity balancing or on human energy and how it can be brought into balance, but mentioned in a profound way is the fact that energy is indestructible. Nikola Tesla, Dr. Judy Wood and other scientists more recently have tried to teach us that. Writing from the trans-Himalayan region of Tibet where the Masters are said to have their private abode, Master Morya wrote to Sinnett in 1882 of the "indestructibility" of energy or what he also terms pure Spirit or "eternal Essence." Humans, over hundreds of years, have labeled this Essence-energy "the Force" or "God" as it has suited them to describe it. Nevertheless, this supreme energy operates by Law that is far superior to any commandants, which means again these Laws cannot be broken, as the Ten Commandants are usually broken by humans everyday, all day, some where on earth. Master Morya wrote to Sinnett about the urgency of polarity balance when he described "electrometers" being used by chelas who "come the whole day to recuperate their nascent powers.," [143] He says cogently more: "The chelas are magnetized..." Moreover, the energy that pours into them is never diminished for it is everlasting. "It is neither a conversion nor creation, but something for which science has yet no name." Fully worth underscoring is that what Master Morya is explaining to Sinnett here is inherently the same message the extraterrestrial RA gave to the group in Kentucky in the early 1980s: energy can be used and manipulated; humans have a lot of distortions to overcome. We need to get to work urgently to overcome the disjuncts, distortions—unsavory energy. We need to work toward balance, as one of the keys to accessing the Source of all and everything. Perhaps not so strange, relatively, is the validation of what the Mahatma said coming from RA, the extraterrestrial mentioned earlier who suggested magnetized water for humans. All forms of balance are foundation keys to expand consciousness and also to optimum health and longevity. The balance between internal programming and external programming is also of prime importance toward achieving what has been called eternal life. For those who need even more evidence that these messages are essential, note that a contemporary science magazine recently mentioned that the genetic code can be tweaked. There are artificial ways of augmenting genetic structure.[144] Gurdjieff was also suggesting that we can augment or shift the programming that is ingrained in us. We must first realize the situation, ponder it carefully and then set to work out of it. What all of this means, again, is that the positive and negative poles must be calibrated, brought together just right. Our mission is to rise up and out of the yin and yang of our very existence. Our Work is to ultimately overcome planetary forces. The human body, mind and spirit must be brought into balance; this is the foundation for overcoming whatever has been programmed into it, from both internal and external sources. It amazes me that so few humans in the West are familiar with the concept of the need to balance Qi or energy in the human body, mind, spirit. Practices to balance energy have been part and parcel of some segments of Asian cultures for thousands of years. Likewise, balancing energy was an essential aspect of ancient Egypt's highest god-like beings. As Jason Quitt has reminded us recently: "we live in an open energy system where we are constantly receiving, transmitting, connecting and communicating with our inner and outer worlds…" [145] "As above, so below!" Energy is indeed available to us from inside the earth and from cosmic realms. A human body in perfect balance manufactures its own high level sustaining energy. Quitt, who knows a lot about Egyptian practices of energy balancing, is another who reminds us that "being in perfect alignment heals, transforms and expands our consciousness…" All of this is also akin to the teachings of Edgar Casey (1877–1945) and Nikola Tesla (1853–1943). Both master intuitive Casey and electrical engineer Tesla expounded the importance of energetic-vibrational balancing. Mentioned in over 1,000 of Casey's psychic readings was the need to tune and enhance the vibratory forces of the human body. Casey's Radiac appliance is still on the market today and widely used. Likewise, Tesla was a proponent of stimulating the healing energies of the body with a vibrational coil which he developed. With vastly different ethnic backgrounds and training, it is a remarkably curious fact that the Mahatmas, Quitt, Casey, Tesla and Gurdjieff all point to the profoundly urgent need for vibrational balance of humans and this is also echoed in a sacred, mostly veiled document, *The Emerald Tablets*. Added to these facts, defibrillation electrode devices are essentially electricity enhancing mechanisms, used successfully in emergency medicine to revive humans for many years. Undoubtedly, electricity is an important component to all living things, including plants and animals.

In his *Meditations,* the masterpiece of Roman Emperor Marcus Aurelius, we are shown multiple times the importance of working for a calm, dispassionate existence, above fray and selfish interests. A Stoic, Aurelius reminded us that history does repeat itself, "everything which happens, always happened so and will happen so…" [146] Aurelius reminded us that our true work is to do "nothing inconsiderately, not without purpose." The quest for calm and balance were replete themes throughout the *Meditations.* Obviously, the true mettle of Marcus Aurelius was reached, not when he was victorious on the battlefield, but when he was gifted with the vision to realize the importance of calm and careful work to overcome. Although he only hints at the real aim of his *Meditations,* from this remove, it is certain he wanted us to know that as we become calm and detached, not careless however, we amass the opportunity to rewrite our human script, to reboot the computer in a manner of speaking.

The supreme validation needed for the purposes here—
that is to provide the most strident credence to the teachings of
Gurdjieff, is as we have been reminded previously: the "secret"
of the 12th Tablet of *The Emerald Tablets*.[147] We note again the
utter uniqueness of this book and are reminded that permission is not granted for a wholesale recount of the *Tablets*, but
more brief summary of number 12 will serve good purpose
here. This particular tablet gives specific instructions to the
initiate on how to rise up, above the strictures of earth time.
Naturally calming the mind and bringing emotions into balance are essential because the mind is the arbiter of the Law
of Cause and Effect; obviously emotion follows little human
minds. When emotions come into play, humans tend to do
unsavory stuff like over eat, blurt "f" words, gossip about
others and even murder each other. Earthlings are prone to
anxieties; learning to meditate has been proven to help under
ordinary circumstances. If medication and professional help
are warranted, this is usually a signal that distortions are really
flawed. Calibration is not easy. Group work can be of great
benefit when the effort is pure and sincere. Meditation helps
tremendously to promote optimum electricity in the body
but also aids in the vibratory quality of the flow of life force.

But it takes years to perfect and is difficult to achieve in its purest form. Sitting quietly every day for a few minutes with no stimulation of cell phones or other electronics is a beginning. Balanced poles are also essential, for this enables magnetism which moves thru nerve paths and is the carrier of all energies to the cells and tissues. The ***Tablets*** promise that an evolved, balanced human can be shown the upper realms and can moreover become free of the barriers of the earth-plane because we are bound to the body—more specifically in our human bodies we are in "bondage."[148]

But even more validation about these matters might be useful for skeptics. My search to find additional evidence from contemporary sources about the wonders of biomagnetism in the quest for balance was fruitful. The mission was to find out if there was any scientific basis for what RA and the Mahatmas taught. RA's intriguing advice to humans that we should drink magnetic water was short and without too much explanation as to how much, why or how often we should sip polarized water. Intuitively, I did not doubt the advice, but still wanted contemporary confirmation perhaps mostly for readers of this essay. It was easy to find and in fact was already in my home library. Ghanshyam Singh Birla and Colette

Hemlin's book *Magnet Therapy* explains that water that has been magnetized is good for tissue reconstruction, strengthens the immune system, eliminates toxins and also reduces cholesterol.[149] The warning is that pregnant women and those with heart conditions should not drink water that has been magnetized. Another expert on biomagnetism, Peter Kulish, teaches us that magnetized water provides two essential elements: oxygen and hydrogen which have overall good benefits for the human body.[150] Oxygen, he reminds us, removes cellular waste and hydrogen controls the "proper functioning of glands and organs." Kulish is a healer whose work has been recognized by the Chinese government, medical professionals and also by officials in the Philippines. Most of us in the West know little about the wonders of vibrational medicine or biomagnetism. It seems not to be built into the core medical school education; and yet I have found one or two physicians who practice "outside the box" of their staunch training. And, now there is a growing number of alternative practitioners of vibrational medicine and biomagnetism and even physicians who are aware of the urgency of balanced biomagnetism. Writing decades ago, Dr. Robert O. Becker revealed in great detail with illustrations, how he used electromagnetism for healing of human fractures, perhaps the first physician trained in the mainstream of Western medicine to provide us with such detailed insight.[151]

The Kybalion is also instructive in our pursuit to understand the nature and importance of balance because this little-known book explains the Laws by which the magnificent, all-knowing, all powerful energy-Essence operates. Humans are orchestrated by Lords who each have a number according to *The Emerald Tablets*. One of these Lords even orchestrates morphology—that is to say the shape, size, anatomical features, voice and all else associated with human anatomy. Another one orchestrates death and determines when, where and how it will happen for each of us. All of this orchestration occurs in an intricate, invisible, unimaginable process, but we surely do see the result. Tablet 3 makes it clear that when humans come to complete balance, "name and form" will "cease to exist in the full light of awakened consciousness."[152] Wow! Whoever put that supreme fact into a sermon that humans could grasp? *The Kybalion* and *The Emerald Tablets* are closely related, because they both give credence to the concept that nothing happens by chance. Where humans are concerned, Cause and Effect is the supreme law that drives our existence, until we adroitly learn our way out of prison. I've come to understand that the Ascended Masters operate as helpers to the Lords of Karma; obviously initiates and chelas operate under and as assistants to Masters. Few of us have ever heard of *The Kybalion* whose author is said to be William Walker Atkinson. The book is based on Hermetic teachings and Hermetic philosophy is based on *The Emerald Tablets*. Atkinson lost practically everything in the carnal world in which we live, but as one follows his biography closely, it is clear that he gained more and more instruction from the spirit world. Providing direct guidance and teaching from a world teacher, T*he Emerald Tablets* render essential lessons of the Egyptian Master deity called Thoth who is also known by some as Tehuti. This deity was born 20,000 years before the sinking of Atlantis. Eventually, the teachings became known as Hermetic philosophy, proffered by Hermes Trismegitus who was likely a reincarnation of Thoth. According to Philip Deslippe, Atkinson's biographer, this unusual human was born in 1862 and grew up in Baltimore, Maryland. Atkinson wrote under several names over many years and was known in theosophy circles, but eventually, near the end of life, he wrote *The Seven Cosmic Laws*. These unbreakable laws are now contained and explained in the book known as *The Kybalion.*[153] The earliest editions do not bear his name because he wrote under the pseudonym, "Three Initiates." Cosmic Laws, as outlined and explained by Atkinson, also support the need to work for balance. For instance, the Cosmic Law of Rhythm or Periodicity reminds humans that we're on a wheel of sorts—whirling electrons, or the undulations of electronic waves"[154] and essentially, we will be incarnated in various forms until we get the lessons we are supposed to get. Atkinson proves his points about this and for me it has become a sad no brainer—a saga of human existence: we are going around in circles. Over lifetimes, continued failure to achieve balance and to grow up to the vertical life, means we will in all likelihood eventually be reduced to the animal kingdom, or perhaps worse, demoted to the mineral kingdom, down there with rocks and what the gospels call brimstone, but there is a hierarchy even to this world. Some rocks and minerals are better and more powerful than others. And, so it is within the human kingdom. In his book *The Theory of Eternal Life*, Rodney Collin provided keen understanding of the different worlds to be navigated by humans.[155] Mental transmutation is the offspring of the Law of Polarity, for if the universal is mental in its nature then, Atkinson says mental transmutation "must be the art of changing the conditions of the universe." This feat is possible when an individual observes himself fully and makes effort toward mentally moving all the way to the opposite side of negative thinking and wrongheaded behaviors. Significant effort made in this pursuit begins the process of growth toward higher consciousness. This is part and parcel of Gurdjieff's teachings.

Keeping to the point that Cosmic Laws support the need for balance, we might use Atkinson as our guide to gaze at the Law of Polarity. Everything on earth seems to appear as opposites. We like something or do not like it. We want something or do not want it. Humans are pulled—sometimes jerked it seems—toward awful behaviors. We seem always to be affirming or denying something or someone. This is the process of planetary forces bearing down on us; it is the stuff of past life Karma. How about having the will to resist these forces, a mental and practical requiem from it all? Little attention is paid to that these days; almost everybody has a big opinion about something. The winner where higher consciousness is concerned is the human who can rest beyond or above affirming or denying, just quietly above it all. We must try harder to overcome the fray and upsets of human life. It is never about "them" in our lives and all of the conflict mustered by others, it is about YOU not getting sucked into unsavory energy. We each have our own Karma and stuff to work off; none of us can peel off layers of wrong doing for someone else. For to die is a singular experience; we must learn to do it right. If we can manage to wake up enough to start serious work before the body breaks down to dust, the blood changes, the vibration changes, everything changes toward everlasting life. This most magnificent process is symbolized in the lovely natural spirals of red rose petals. The red rose is the exemplar of perfection, it signals something mostly unknown to medical science. From outside, as a gift from the Source of all and everything, the human blood actually changes when one is awake enough to be calibrated and securely on the path to higher consciousness. As witnessed in this chapter and the last, the gospels only hint that it is the blood that saves us without giving a full explanation.

Some of us have attended church services which offer the sacrament of drinking wine that is symbolic of the blood of Christ. In the church where I grew up, we drank symbolic grape juice which my aunt, secretary to the minister, dutifully purchased and stored for the ritual. Some of us globally take away wrong signals or misinformation from these practices and assume that it is really the blood of Christ that leads to or ensures that each of us will automatically gain eternal life. To understand this way is simply wrongheaded. The rituals are purely symbolic as is the practice of drinking wine or grape juice is symbolic of the blood of Christ. Again and again somebody needs to remind us that we each must do actual grunt Work on ourselves and definitely do no harm to others. In short, we each must rescue ourselves and tread earth life carefully. Then and only then can the atonement process begin. Dr. Vesey enlightened us about some of the process in **The Spiritual Mysteries of Blood**, and let us not forget, likewise, Trevor Ravenscroft who described the starting point of connection to higher consciousness is most assuredly with "etherization" of the blood. Medical science cannot see this except that it has been acknowledged that the blood of some of us as we age is different than the blood of most elderly. The point for us to hold here is that red is the color on the spectrum of vibration that signals this process has begun. No wonder the rose is accompanied by thorns which seem to stand guard over this indomitable, precious flower. Thus, to know the real meaning of the rose is to come full circle to the meaning of the epigraph borrowed from T.S. Eliot which opens this essay: to summon the spectre of the rose it is essential to let go of "antique drums"—that is to say the past—and to die to the old self. We must be better, do better, quiet down and perfect meditation practices as we actually make willful effort toward eternal life. Now more than ever, with the global COVID scare and heightened anxiety over vaccines, daily regular practices of quieting the mind and focusing on breathing with pure intent to achieve stillness are essential. All of this is not easy, but from my perspective, is clearly preferred to taking chances on stepping into the great abyss having done no higher consciousness Work at all.

[1]   For example, the Girlfriends, Inc., an American-based mostly social and civic minded group has used the rose as a symbol since the organization was founded in 1932. So have other organizations and fraternal orders such as the Golden Dawn and the Rosicrucian orders worldwide.

[2]   The Island of Rhodes in Greece used the rose as a symbol on coins in 1200 B.C.

[3]   For instance, the movie "V is for Vendetta" in which rose petals are used as a powerful symbol of good overcoming evil. Starring Natalie Portman and Hugo Weaving and directed by James McTeigue, "V" was released in 2006.

[4]   In Nandor Fodor's, *Between Two Worlds* (Parker Publishing Company, West Nyack, New York) see Chapter Two "*The Riddle of Vaslav Nijinsky*" that describes Nijinsky's superior dance skills and levitation in the ballet "Secret Rose." On page 22, it is described how "Nijinsky possessed the ability to remain in the air at the highest point of elevation before descending." Although Nijinsky suffered from mental illness later in his life, he is known to have had unusual talent connected to dance feats.

[5]   See for instance, see Umberto Echo's *The Name of the Rose,* Hartcourt Brace & Company (New York) 1980, a well researched work of fiction and also the movie based on the this title staring Sean Connery and Christian Slater.

[6]   Barbara Seward, *The Symbolic Rose*, Spring Publications, Inc., Dallas, Texas, 1954, p. 37.

7   Helen M. Luke, *Dark Wood to White Rose: A Study of Meanings in Dante's Divine Comedy*, (Dove Publications, Pecos, New Mexico) 1975, p.11.

8   Luke, *Dark Wood to White Rose*, p. 11.

9   Dante Alighieri's *Divine Comedy* Translated by H. F. Cary in *Classics Appreciation Society Condensations*, Grolier, Inc. 1955, p. 451.

10   Ibid., p.444.

11   Ibid., p.444.

12   Dante Alighieri, *The Inferno*, Translated By Henry Wadsworth Longfellow, Introduction and Notes By Peter Bondanella, (New York, Barnes and Noble Classics, 2003), p.xxxi

13   Ibid., xxxv.

14   Barbara Seward, *The Symbolic Rose*, p. 156.

15   Ibid, p.89.

16   Ibid., p. 89.

17   Richard Cavendish, *A History of Magic* (New York Arkana, Division of Penguin Books, 1990) p. 142.

18   *Introducing the Theosophical Society,* Wheaton, Illinois. http://www.theosophical.org.

19   R.Cavendish, *A History of Magic,* p.146.

20   Colin Wilson, *The Occult,* p. 416–417.

21   Thomas D. Worrel, "A Brief Study of the Rose Cross Symbol," publisher and date unknown, p. 3.

22   Paul Foster Case, *The True and Invisible Rosicrucian Order: An Interpretation of the Rosicrucian Allegory and An Explanation of the Ten Rosicrucian Grades.* Weiser Books, Boston, 1985, p. 4.

23   Ibid., p. 5.

24   Mastery of Life, publication of the Supreme Grand Lodge of the Ancient & Mystical Order Rosae Crucis, AMORC, Inc. p.7.

25   Worrel, "A Brief Study of the Rose Cross Symbol", p.2.

26   Ibid., p.2

27   Lynn Picknett and Clive Prince, *The Templar Revelation: Secret Guardians of the True Identity of Christ, Touchstone,* New York, 1997, p.134.

28   Ibid., p. 135.

29   Isreal Regardie, *The Golden Dawn: A Complete Course in Ceremonial Magic*; Four Volumes in One, (St. Paul, Minnesota, Llewellyn Publications, 1986) p. 310.

30   James Pethica, ed. Yeats Poetry, Drama and Prose *"From The Secret Rose, 1897"* Norton Publishing, New York, 2000, p. 195.

31   Ibid.

32   Ibid. p.197.

33   Coleman Barks et. el. Translators, *The Essential Rumi,* Castle Books, Edison, New Jersey, 1997, introduction.

34   Ibid. p. 37.

35   Ibid. p. 38.

36   Ibid. p. 212.

37   Ibid., p. 212.

38   Hakim Sanai, The Walled Garden of Truth, Translated and Abridged by D. L. Pendlebury, (The Octagon Press, London, England) p. 7.

39   Ibid., p. 37.

40   Ibid., p. 8.

41   Hidden knowledge and the secret teachings of Jesus are mentioned and alluded to throughout *The Holy Bible*, including in Mark 4:11 which says "Unto you it is given to know the Kingdom of God: but unto them that are without, all these things are done in parables." That is to say many people worldwide read the Bible, but very few fully understand it. It is a tremendously complex book that takes years of study, reflection, and pure intent to understand. This too is made clear in the Book of Mark, Chapter 4, verse 12: "Seeing they may see and not perceive; and hearing they may hear and

not understand; lest at any time they should be converted and their sins should be forgiven them."

[42] Rudolf Borchardt, The Passionate Gardener, English Translation by Henry Martin (Kingston, New York, McPherson Publishing, 2006), p.8.

[43] Mechthild Scheffer, *Bach Flower Therapy*, (Rochester, VT, Healing Arts Press, 1988), p. 16–17.

[44] Ibid., p. 16.

[45] Edward Bach and F. J. Wheeler, *Bach Flower Remedies*, (New Canaan, CT, Keats Publishing, Inc. 1997), p. 7.

[46] Ibid.

[47] Peter Lemesurier, *The Unknown Nostradamus*, John Hunt Publishing Ltd., 2003, p. 62.

[48] Ian Wilson, *Nostradamus: The Man Behind the Prophecies*, p. 45.

[49] Facts provided by Hisae Ogawa in translation from Dr. Harada's Japanese writings to English from: *Moment of Peace* (date unknown), Gariver Products Co, Ltd. *Hiroshima Roses* (1989) Mirai-sha Publisher; and *Chasing the Dream of Peace* (1983), Kei-shobo Publisher, Japan.

[50] Geoffrey Hodson, *The Hidden Wisdom in the Holy Bible*, Volume I, (Wheaton, Ill. The Theosophical Publishing House, 1963), p. 129.

[51] Kenneth W. Osbeck, *101 Hymn Stories*, (Grand Rapids, Michigan, 1982), p. 124.

[52] *New York Times*, March 12, 1946, p. 26.

[53] Ibid.

[54] Of interest is Jeremy Scahill's book *Blackwater: The Rise of the World's Most Powerful Mercenary Army* (New York City, Avalon Books, 2007).

[55] Ann Applebaum, *Gulag*, (New York City, Penguin Books, 2006), p. 177.

[56] Hans Biedermann, *Dictionary of Symbolism: Cultural Icons and the Meanings Behind Them*. (New York, Penguin Books, USA, Inc. 1992), p. 290.

[57]   Marcell Jankovics, *Book of the Sun* translated and edited by Mario Fenyo (Wayne, NJ Hungarian Studies Publications, Inc. and Columbia University Press, 2001),p. 110.

[58]   Donald Tyson, editor, *Three Books of Occult Philosophy: Written by Henry Cornelius, Completely Annotated with Modern Commentary; The Foundation Book of Western Occultism*, (St. Paul, MN, 2004), p.132.

[59]   For more on the rose nebula, see Jerry Bonnell and Robert J. Nemiroff's *Astronomy 365 Days: The Best of the Astronomy Picture of the Day Website*, (Abrams, New York, 2006). Also of interest is *Constellations, Stars and Celestial Objects*, (Firefly Books, Stuttgart, Germany, 2005)

[60]   Rudiger Dahlke, *Mandalas of the World: A Meditating and Painting Guide*, (New York, Sterling Publishing Co., Inc. 2001), p.136.

[61]   *The Christian Holy Bible* has had numerous translations and versions and not all elect to use the rose in metaphor, but the most widely used King James version does mention the rose in the books of <u>Isaiah</u> and Song of Songs. The Holy Bible: New International Version makes reference to the crocus instead of the rose in the book of *Isaiah*, Chapter 35. Interestingly, the King James version is thought by some to have been written by Francis Bacon on behalf of King James I of England; this notion is feasible since Bacon was steeped in Masonic and metaphysical traditions and is even thought to be the true author of Shakespeare's plays and sonnets that are also full of parable and allegory that reference the divine.

[62]   Israel Regardie, *The Golden Dawn: A Complete Course in Practical Ceremonial Magic* (St. Paul, Minnesota, Llewllyn Publications, 1986), p. 47.

[63]   Jacob Needleman, *Why Can't We Be Good?* (New York, Penguin Group, 2007), p. 252. Needleman is the author of several books related to mysticism, including *Introduction to The Gurdjieff Work*, 2013.

[64] *The Secret of the Golden Flower*: A Chinese Book of Life Translated and explained by Richard Wilhelm with Commentary by Dr. C. J. Jung, (New York, Harcourt Brace Javannovich, 1931), p. viii.

[65] See Norman Mailer's book, <u>On God</u>, (New York, Random House, 2007).

[66] To corroborate this notion of war, weapons and conflict at the bidding of government, see, for instance, *Blackwater USA*, 2007 that explains the development of a private military force.

[67] Leo Tolstoy, *The Kingdom of God is Within You: Christianity Not as a Mystic Religion But As A New Theory of Life,* Martin Green, editor, (Lincoln, Nebraska, University of Nebraska Press, 1984), p. 152.

[68] Mark Lilla, "The Politics of God," *New York Times Magazine,* August 19, 2007, p.30.

[69] In this regard, See Jim Marr's book *The Secret War* (New York, Random House, 2003) and Anna Politkovskaya's *Putin's Russia* (London: The Harville Press, 2004).

[70] Mark Lilla, *"The Politics of God",* p.50.

[71] Of interest is a symphony produced in Rumi's honor by Hafez Nazeri during this 800th year celebration of his birth and the United Nations declaration of 2007 as the International Year of Rumi. In September 2007, the University of Maryland's Center for Persian Studies, College Park, MD sponsored a 3-day event honoring the work of Rumi. See *The Washington Post,* August 30, 2007, p. C6.

[72] As quoted in Manly P. Hall, *The Teachings of All Ages,* (New York, Penguin Group, 2003), p.347.

[73] David Stewart, *The Chemistry of Essential Oils: God's Love Manifest in Molecules* (Marble Hill, MO., Care Publications, 2006) p. 153.

[74] John Ballou Newbrough, *OAHSPE, A New Bible in the Words of Jehovih and His Angel Embassadors,* (London, England, Kosmon Press, 1942) p. iv.

[75] Read Elisabeth Haich's account in *Initiation*, (Santa Fe, NM, Aurora Press, 2000).

[76] OAHSPE, p. v.

[77] OAHSPE, Book of Jehovih's Kingdom on Earth, Chapter VIII, Verse 8, p. 814.

[78] OAHSPE, Book of Jehovih's Kingdom…, Chapter XI, Verse 29, p. 818

[79] OAHSPE, Book of Discipline, Chapter III, Verse 14, p. 837.

[80] OAHSPE, Book of Saphah, p. 618.

[81] See C.W. Leadbeater's *The Chakras* first published in 1927 by Quest Books, Wheaton, Illinois and now in its 9th printing. On page 7, Leadbeater notes that there are seven charkas. Also of interest is Ruth White's *Using Your Chakras: A New Approach to Healing Your Life* (New York: Barnes and Noble, 1998)

[82] Regarding remote viewing, of interest are Paul H. Smith's *Reading The Enemy's Mind: Inside Star Gate* (New York: Published by Tom Doherty Associates, 2005) and Jim Schnabel's *Remote Viewing: The Secret History of America's Psychic Spies* (New York, Bantam, Doubleday Dell Publishing, 1997)

[83] Lee Priestly, *SHALAM; Utopia on the Rio Grande, 1881–1907*, (El Paso, Texas Western Press, 1988), p.32.

[84] Ibid., p.33.

[85] Ibid., p.22.

[86] Countess Constance Wachtmeister et al., *Reminiscences of H. P. Blavatsky and the Secret Doctrine*, Wheaton Illinois, Theosophical Publishing House, 1976.

[87] Master DK or Djwhal Khul is said to have been HPB's guide or master. Of interest regarding ascended masters is Phillip Lindsay's book, *Masters of the Seven Rays: Their Past Lives and Reappearance* (Queensland, Australia, Apollo Publishing, 2006), p.49.

88   Ibid., p. 41.

89   Mary K. Neff, editor, Personal Memoirs of H. P. Blavatasky (New York, E. P. Dutton & Co., Inc. 1937), p. 37.

90   Ibid., p. 26.

91   Manly Hall, editor, *The Phoenix: An Illustrated Review of Occultism and Philosophy* (Los Angeles, Hall Publishing, Co., 1931–32 edition), p. 86.

92   Noteworthy is Lewis Spence's *The History of Atlantis* originally published in 1926 by Rider & Son, London and New York. Plato's work, *Timaeus* was published 400 years before the birth of Christ.

93   See H. P. Blavatsky's *The Secret Doctrine: The Synthesis of Science, Religion and Philosophy, Volume II, Anthropogenesis*_(London, Theosophical Publishing Company, 1888), p 333.

94   See Erich von Daniken's film *"Chariots of the Gods"* released in 1972 by Sun Classic Pictures and packaged in 2005 by Blair and Associates, Ltd. Von Daniken's controversial theory is that man did not descend from apes as maintained by Charles Darwin, but that humans have descended from gods.

95   Michael Doreal, *An Interpretation of the Emerald Tablets Together With The Two Extra Tablets*, (Castle Rock, CO. Brotherhood of the White Temple), p. 8

96   Whitby, Delores, <u>Doreal</u>: *As I Knew Him* (Sedalia, CO., Little Temple Library, 1980), p. 5.

97   Ibid., p. 15.

98   *The Emerald Tablets*, p.132.

99   R.A. Charles, editor, *The Book of Enoch* (San Diego, CA, The Book Tree 1917, 2006)p. 91. Another reference appears on page 64.

100   The Bible has been altered and translated a number of times. That this is a fact has been noted by a number of scholars. In The Teachings of All Ages, page 543, for example, Manly P.Hall explains that regarding the King James version, Sir Francis Bacon was the translator given the task

of checking, editing and revising the Scriptures. According to Hall, the very first edition of the King James version contains a cryptic Baconian headpiece. Interestingly, Phillip Lindsay in *Masters of the Seven Rays* notes that Francis Bacon "wrote secret ciphers …for the Holy Bible [King James version] and [for] Shakespearean plays; see p. 29.

101   *Holy Bible King James Study Bible*, Thomas Nelson Publishers, (Nashville, 1988)1010. The interpretations from this version are divided thusly: (1) allegorical: treats the view of early Jewish literature, denies the literal aspects (2) Typological:: in this view marriage is seen as a type of Christ and the Church (3) Collection of love songs: says the Song of Solomon is just love songs with no unified meaning (4) Love Triangle: that song of Solomon is about the love triangle or "eternal triangle" with Solomon as the villain who tried to lure the maiden from her shepherd-boyfriend and (5) Literal love story: view that this book is just that, a love saga.

102   Hidden knowledge and the secret teachings of Jesus are mentioned and alluded to throughout *The Bible,* including in Mark 4:11 which says "Unto you it is given to know the Kingdom of God: but unto them that are without, all these things are done in parables." That is to say many people worldwide read the Bible, but very few fully understand it. It is a tremendously complex book that takes years of study, reflection, and sincere intent to understand. This is also made clear in the Book of Mark, Chapter 4, verse 12: "Seeing they may see and not perceive; and hearing they may hear and not understand; lest at any time they should be converted and their sins should be forgiven them."

103   This knowledge is replete in *The Christian Holy Bible*, sometimes in allegory, sometimes clearly stated such as in Mark 1:4 "I baptize you with water, but he will baptize you with the Holy Spirit" and in Mark 3:28, "… But whoever blasphemes against the Holy Spirit will never be forgiven; he is guilty of an eternal sin." In fact, there are over 60 references to the Holy

Spirit or Holy Ghost in the King James version of *The Holy Bible*. One can only guess at the number of times it is mentioned in numerous other versions.

[104] Beverly Moon, editor The Encyclopedia of Archetypical Symbolism: The Archive for Research in Archtypical Symbolism, London, Shambhala, 1991),p.308.

[105] See Marcell Jankovich, *Book of the Sun*, p. 120. Also of interest is Mel Gibson's movie, "*Apocolypto*" (2006) that graphically depicts the practice of human sacrifice during the Aztec empire of the 15th century.

[106] Michael Doreal, *An Interpretation of the Emerald Tablets*, p. 49.

[107] Hargrove Jennings, p.111

[108] Philip Ball, *The Devil's Doctor: Paracelsus and the World of Renaissance Magic and Science* (Farrar, Straus and Giroux, 2006), p. 124.

[109] Ibid., p. 124.

[110] Of interest is Evelyn Underhill's classic book **Mysticism** which describes a personal process toward spiritual consciousness and gives examples of what to expect, Meridian Books, New York, 1955.

[111] See George I. Gurdjieff's book, known as the Third Series, **Life Is Real, Then, Only When' I Am'**

[112] Ponder this with regard to the symbol of the cross in the Christian tradition. The vertical line represents the Holy Spirit or the potential for humans to rise up so as to be met by spirit which is possible when the time is right. The horizontal line represents the limits of the material, time-driven world in which the vast majority of humans seem mired.

[113] See Gurdjieff's specific commentary on third world citizenship in **Life is Real, Only, Then, When "I Am"**, p. 173, known widely among students of Gurdjieff as the Third Series, published by Pearson, Arkana, New York,1975, 1978, 1991, with forward by Jeanne De Salzmann.

114   See chapter IV "The Sacred and Non-Sacred Planets" for complete explanation of the nature of the planets in Alice Bailey's *Esoteric Astrology*, Lucis Publishing, New York, 1951. p. 503–533.

115   Paul Beekman Taylor, *Gurdjieff's America: Mediating the Miraculous*, Lighthouse Editions Limited, www.lighthouse-editions.com, 2004. Dr. Taylor recounts many of the trials and tribulations of Gurdjieff's endeavor to bring his unique way of teaching metaphysics to America.

116   Elisabeth Haich, *Initiation,* p. 153.

117   See for instance, Jim Marrs book *Alien Agenda: Investigating the Extraterrestrial Presence Among Us*, (New York, Harper Collins, 1997); also of interest in this regard is Zecharia Sitchin's book *The Lost Realms* and Chris Hardy's *The DNA of the Gods*.

118   Chris H. Hardy, *DNA of the Gods: The Anunnaki Creation of Eve and the Alien Battle for Humanity*, Bear and Company, (Rochester, Vermont, 2014). Ninmah the goddess who perfected humans is said to have worn traditional headdress with two horns of a bull or cow, which Dr. Hardy suggests is the reason so many in India revere the cow and how we came to use the expression "sacred cow."

119   Noteworthy is Thomas Walker's article "A Path With Heart" in *Quest*, Spring, 2010, p. 55–59 which recalls case studies which substantiate unseen, intelligent energy information operating in the tissue of every organ; cellular memory is now a scientific fact.

120   For instance, notice the recent increase in the murder rate now and armed conflicts, but these have been part and parcel of human nature in every epoch, globally. Humans get more and more creative in their use of violence toward themselves and others. USA Today notes, October 27, 2016, a recent rise in "drugged driving." See "A Spate of drugged driving deaths alarms U.S. regulators" which points to over 31,000 auto deaths associated with drug use and "Poll: 51% fear Election Day violence." How is it that

violence is being discussed in a headline on the front page, even before the election occurs?

[121] G.I. Gurdjieff, *Beelzebub's Tales to His Grandson*, All and Everything First Series, (New York, Penguin, 1964), p.88

[122] See *OAHSPE*, "Book of Openta-Armij, Daughter of Jehovih" verse 25, p. 319.

[123] Instructive about this almost unimaginable process is Gurdjieff's chapter in the *Tales*, entitled Chapter 45, "In the Opinion of Beelzebub, Man's Extraction of Electricity from Nature and Its Destruction During Its Use, Is One of the Chief Causes of Shortening of the Life of Man," pages 1145–1160.

[124] Ocke de Boer, *Higher Being Bodies: A Non-Dualistic Approach to the Fourth Way, With Hope*, Beech Hill Publishing Company, (Mount Desert, Maine), see page 2 where Ocke reminds us that solar coating takes a very long time, "it cannot be done in one lifetime."

[125] G. I. Gurdjieff, *Beelzebub's Tales to His Grandson*, Penguin Books (New York, 1964, 1999), see page **217.** Also, noteworthy is the mention of "roses, roses" on page 433, but this latter reference is not in the same vein as the first. The first reference being the essential one because here the flower is connected directly to "GOD" and thus has been put in capital letters.

[126] Farid Ud-Din Attar, *The Conference of the Birds*, translated by Afkham Darbandi and Dick Davis, Penguin Books, (London, England), p. 36, lines 755–75. {Here the rose is a metaphor for the Holy Sprit, apparently well known by the mysterious man in the poem.}

[127] Attar, *The Conference of the Birds*, p.36.

[128] See the last Chapter of Gurdjieff's *Life is Real*, p. 173.

[129] G. I. Gurdjieff, *Beelzebub's Tales to His Grandson*, p.349.

[130] Gurdjieff, *Beelzebub's Tales...*, p. 348.

[131] *The Emerald Tablets*.

[132] Trevor Ravenscroft, *The Spear of Destiny*, Samuel Weiser, Inc. (York Beach, Maine, 1973), see pages 238 where Ravenscroft explains the necessity for humans to become "fully expanded etheric organisms" by letting go of all selfish cravings and desires. Also, page. 251.

[133] Ravenscroft, *The Spear of Destiny*, see the introduction.

[134] Don Elkins, Carla Rueckert, James Allen McCarty, *The Law of One: Book 1, The RA Material, An Ancient Astronaut Speaks* (Whitford Press, Atglen, PA., 1984), p.65.

[135] See, for instance A.T. Mann's *Life Time Astrology: From Conception to Transcendence*, Allen and Unwin Publishers, 1984; subsequently published in the UK 1991, Element Books, Dorset. Also of interest is Montgomery Taylor's essay in *Rose Lore*, Third Edition (2015) entitled "The Rose and Astrology" p.110–120, which reminds us that in years past natal astrology was reserved for royalty and a select few. Commoners rarely knew their birthdates and times which is essential information for an accurate charting.

[136] *The Tibetan Book of the Dead, translation by Robert A.F. Thurman, Bantam, New York, 1994, p. 18.*

[137] Richard Smoley, "The Mystery of the Seven Seals," in *Quest Magazine*, Spring 2017.

[138] Farid UD-Din Attar*, The Conference of the Birds*, translated by Afkham Darbani and Dick Davis, Penguin Books, (1984), 141–142.

[139] Martin Schonberger*, The I- Ching and the Genetic Code*, Aurora Press, Santa Fe, NM (2004), p.21.

[140] Don Elkins, et el., *The Law of One: Book I, The RA Material*, p.127.

[141] George I. Gurdjieff, *Life is Real, Then Only When I Am, p.173.* (The most auspicious chapter is the final unfinished writing in this work, "*The Outer and Inner World of Man.*")

[142]   Dante Alighieri, *The Divine Comedy*, Part 3, Paradise, inside Grolier Classics (1955), p. 560.

[143]   *The Mahatma Letters to A. P. Sinnett*, transcribed, Compiled by A.T. Barker, First Edition, 1923 (Theosophical University Press), p. 61–62.

[144]   *Popular Science*, Special Edition "Future Body," Fall 2018, p. 72.

[145]   Jason Quitt and Saundra Arnold,*: Ancient Egyptian QiGong System, Egyptian Postures of Power*, publisher unknown; www.thecrystalsun.com.

[146]   *Meditations of Marcus Aurelius* translated by George Long, in Condensation by Grolier Classics, 1956, p. 437.

[147]   The *Emerald Tablets. Of Thoth-The-Atlantean: An Interpretation of Emerald Tablets* by Dr. Doreal, Brotherhood of the White Temple, Inc., 2002, p. 173–76. (Please note: several books have been titled "Emerald Tablets," but this authentic version is so extraordinary that it will not permit readers to tackle it to completion until their vibration is lifted; it can be acquired only thru the Brotherhood of the White Temple or from a student of the Brotherhood.)

[148]   *The Emerald Tablets*, p. 174.

[149]   Ghanshyam Singh Birla and Colette Hemlin, *Magnet Therapy*, Healing Arts Press, Rochester, Vermont, 1999, p. 108–109.

[150]   Peter Kulish, *Conquering Pain: The Art of Healing with BioMagnetism*, Fountainville Press, 1999, p.26–27.

[151]   Robert O. Becker, MD and Gary Selden, *The Body Electric: Electromagnetism and the Foundation of Life*, (New York), 1985.

[152]   *The Emerald Tablets*, p. 127.

[153]   William Walker Atkinson, *The Kybalion: The Definitive Edition, introduced by Philip Deslippe, Tarcher/Penguin (2008).*

[154]   Atkinson, *The Kybalion*, p. 273.

[155]   Rodney Collin, *The Theory of Eternal Life*, Mercury Publications, Sun Valley, Texas, (2006).

ROSE PARADISE BRIEF INDEX

ABOUT THE AUTHOR

*Frankie Pauling Hutton is a former journalist, historian, and collegiate professor whose scholarly books have been used widely in the academy in America and abroad. **Rose Paradise**, a uniquely metaphysical rendering, culls from and is a companion to her earlier book **Rose Lore: Essays in Cultural History and Semiotics** which has been published in the United States and abroad in China and Europe.*

Dr. Hutton grew up in a staunchly Christian tradition, but has travelled the globe to study with Kabbalists, Taoists and with Gurdjieff, Theosophical and other esoteric groups, thus her insight and understanding is discerned and enriched by all of these traditions. She has been a Salzburg Fellow, has taught intellectual history at the collegiate level and worked in course development at a United States military chaplain school.